Dedicated to
everyone here and in overseas
who loves the freedom of others
as much as his or her own.
Who cares and shares.
Who pursues happiness
and finds kindness, safety and truth,
humour, wonders and respect,
justice, wisdom and tenderness,
true solidarity and peace.

Now We Go... Overseas!

Emigration from Hesse
via Bremen to North America

By Monika Felsing

Edited by Susan B. Eldridge

Based on a podcast of the Historical Society
Lastoria, Bremen, in cooperation with volunteers
in the United States and Germany

Bibliografische Information der Deutschen Nationalbibliothek
Die Deutsche Nationalbibliothek verzeichnet diese Publikation
in der Deutschen Nationalbibliografie; detaillierte bibliografische
Daten sind im Internet über www.dnb.de abrufbar.

Covermotiv: Auswandererdenkmal in Bremerhaven.

Gestaltung: Wolfgang Rulfs
www.wolfgang-rulfs.de

Verlag: BoD · Books on Demand GmbH, Überseering 33,
22297 Hamburg, bod@bod.de
Druck: Libri Plureos GmbH, Friedensallee 273, 22763 Hamburg

ISBN: 978-3-7597-9554-0

Content

Let's go!

For uncounted Germans and other Europeans migration was the only way to keep or improve one's life until the 19th and in the 20th century. They left their villages, their hometowns, their countries, the most uncomfortable comfort zones to start anew overseas. In one of its projects, our Historical Society Lastoria, Bremen, has done research, concerning for example early human rights and democracy movement in the 19th Century and refugees of the Nazi era. Historian and journalist Monika Felsing and other volunteers have told the stories of several Jewish and Christian families with roots in Upper Hesse or other parts of Germany and Europe, and got in contact with other researchers, genealogists, institutions and authors.

In 2022, the podcast project "Now we go... Overseas!" of Lastoria started with volunteers in Bremen, Berlin and Hesse. After a year, it became almost overnight a trans-atlantic project, supported by the genealogist Susan Eldridge nee Badenhausen in Connecticut, whose ancestor Edmund Badenhausen from Melsungen had become Capitain in the 19th Century and moved to the U.S. where he was in charge for the peer of Hapag and the Nord-deutsche Lloyd in Hoboken, New Jersey. I have used AI for initial translations of my manuscript from German to English, and Susan Eldridge who had after a short, but understandable hesitation agreed to be the voluntary director of the English version, helped me to revise it, and the book has benefited from her extensive proofreading. A teamwork that I have appreciated and enjoyed very much! Together, we have turned the written words into an audio of several hours, and then, thanks to a good friend, graphic designer Wolfgang Rulfs, into this book.

In libraries and at kitchen tables, volunteers, mostly amateurs, have read the documents, the quotations from literature from the 19th Century, or sang songs, to keep memories alive. Professional musicians played music from various eras and in various styles. A Chanty Choir from Bremen sang a sailor's song, Niki Rittenhouse from Connecticut the English version of the project's theme: "Now we go... Overseas". A brass band from Upper Hesse has contributed "Muss i denn", and several audios from the well-kept archive of Lastoria have been used. Duo Eigenart from Nidderau for example played music from the time of the Social Revolution in Hesse, early 19th Century, on historical instruments at the Weidig weekend in Ober-Gleen in 2015. Klezmer historian and violinist Yale Strom from San Diego introduces the audience to Jewish Music, Burghard Bock from Bremen has interpreted "Di grine kuzine" on the mandolin. Veronika Bloemers from Frankfurt/Main plays a Sabbath song on a grand piano (an instrument by Steinway & Sons, a company founded by Heinrich Engelhardt Steinweg, born in 1797 in Wolfs-hagen in the Harz mountains, not far from Hesse, and emigrated in 1850 with his big family to the U.S.) in the Hohhaus Museum, Lauterbach. And we also proudly present an audio of Henry Smolen, grandson of the refugee Herbert Sondheim, playing Beethoven.

Readers and listeners will learn something about ordinary people's dream of a new life and their contributions to American history, about members of the Giessen Emigration Society who hoped to settle in Missouri and to found, with the support of Americans of German descent, their own democratic German state in the U.S., a place where tolerance, human rights and liberty should rule. The podcast tells the story of some female pioneers in the U.S. and discusses women's rights in the 19th Century. There were Jewish Hessians finding refuge in the U.S. and others who were rejected and sent to concentration camps. We accompany the German journalist Heinrich Lemcke during his visit on Ellis Island in the early 1890s, and ask how immigration laws have changed since.

Our Historical Society Lastoria wishes to thank every volunteer who has participated in this transatlantic project about migration, as well as everyone who has performed the research and published the information from which this was written. The podcast consists of six parts that are online, in the United States at badmorgen.wordpress.com. In Germany you can find them at monikafelsing.de. If you have any questions or want to support our volunteers' work, please don't hesitate to concact us in Germany at mail@lastoria-bremen.de or in the United States at badmorgenealogy@gmail.com.

But now... let's go!

Out of necessity to America

Hessian emigrants in the 19th and early 20th Century

Now we go overseas[1]
(Coversong of the old German folksong "Jetzt fahrn wir übern See")

Now we go overseas, overseas,
now we go over...
Now we go overseas, overseas,
now we go overseas!
On an old sailing vessel, vessel, vessel, vessel,
on an old sailing vessel,
departing hurts so...
On an old sailing vessel, vessel, vessel, vessel,
on an old sailing vessel,
departing hurts so much!

Up and away. The people of Hesse have left their hometowns. They go with their children: far, far away, via Bremen, Bremerhaven some also via Hamburg to America. We want to tell some of their stories and turn back time by a little more than two centuries, not quite to the eight years of the American War of Independence, 1775 to 1783. This is when the Landgraf of Hesse-Kassel rented thou-

---

[1] Coversong of the old German folksong „Jetzt fahrn wir übern See" (meaning: Now we are crossing the lake). The composer and the author of the original lyrics are unknown, it is a game as well as a song, the pauses are intended. The version in Upper Hessian dialect and the English translation have been written by Monika Felsing. There are several stanzas in this chapter.

sands of his male subjects as soldiers to the British and they sang goodbye at the parade in Kassel:[2]

Yay, to America!
To you, Germany, good night!
You Hessians, present your rifle,
the Landgraf is coming to the watch!
Goodbye, Landgraf Friedrich,
you pay us liquor and beer.
If we lose an arm or a leg, if men are shot
England will pay to you.
You lousy rebels, you,
beware of us Hessians!
Yay, to America!
To you, Germany, good night.

Four decades later, the brothers Grimm have collected fairy tales told to them by women in Kassel. One is about four who are sentenced to death and run away, and begins like this: "There was a man with a donkey who had served him faithfully for many years, but whose strength was now running out, so that he became more and more unfit for work. The master not only wanted to cut back on the donkey's food, but he also did not want to feed him anymore. The donkey, noticing that there was no good wind, ran away and made his way to Bremen; there, he thought, you can become a town musician."[3]

---

[2] Song of the Hessian rented soldiers, they sang it at a parade in Kassel on October 19 in 1775.

[3] The beginning of the Town Musicians of Bremen from the "Children's and Household Tales" of 1819, collected by the brothers Grimm. Meanwhile there is an Upper Hessian version in the project "Sprachmusikanten" (language musicians) of the Literaturhaus Bremen: https://www.literaturhaus-bremen.de/sprachmusikanten-bremen/deine-sprache. There are versions in several languages as audios! Fairy tales in Upper Hessian are to be heard in the blog on the website www.monikafelsing.de.

The donkey, the dog, the cat, and the rooster are still mentioned as emigrants in the 1819 edition of the "Children's and Household Tales", even if they did not get far. Not even as far as Bremen, to be exact. Millions of people, however, are driven beyond the borders of today's Germany, to countries about which they know little. Some move overland to the east, to Poland, Lithuania, Russia or Hungary. Others venture across the Atlantic. In 1819, anyone who wanted to leave and could read, and there were very few of them at the time, learned something about the "Ordinance on the Emigration of Subjects to America, in particular the Conduct of the Police Directorate of the Free City of Bremen in the event of unsuccessful emigration projects". Whether deciphered, passed on or read aloud, everything is eagerly devoured.

In March 1835, the Bremen shipowner Friedrich Jacob Wichelhausen placed the following advertisement in the newspaper: "Announcement. All the ships I handled last year with passengers to the United States of America have not only arrived there happily and after a voyage of 35 to a maximum of 45 days, but the passengers have also shown their complete satisfaction with the passage, with the treatment of the ship's captain and the food received on board by a written testimony, which then also prompted me to pay the ship's captains the bonus promised to them in this case. Mr. Werner Ramspeck Junior had the kindness to take over the agency for me in the local area for the acceptance of passengers. And I therefore ask all those who intend to leave for the United States of America this year to turn to this gentleman as soon as possible. The same person is authorized to receive the earnest money for my account and to agree with the passengers on the conditions of the crossing."[4]

Now we go overseas

In the port of Bremerhaven
we went on our...
In the port of Bremerhaven,
we went on our ship!
With all our belongings, longings, longings, longings,
With all our belongings,
we started our...!
With all our belongings, longings, longings, longings,
with all our belongings,
we started our trip!

Some villages even pay for the crossing for their poor and others whom they want to get rid of. In his article on "Emigrants from the parish of Maulbach" in a publication of the Alsfeld Historical Society, Wolfgang Seim gives several examples of this. His most important source was the emigrant lists of Karl Geisel in the city archives of Alsfeld. Among those who left the country at the expense of their home community was the 28-year-old Balthasar, a beggar whom the community of Dannenrod probably sent to his older sister in the United States in 1854. In a profile from 1851 he is described as "mentally weak". A few decades later, the authorities of the United States no longer allow mentally retarded people to enter the country.[5]

---

[4] Advertising in the local newspaper Alsfelder Wochenblatt, March 1835.
[5] The statistics from Großen-Buseck are from Weitershaus about emigration from Upper Hesse, p. 199. The examples from aus Dannenrod, Maulbach et cetera are from Wolfgang Seim's report „Auswanderer aus dem Kirchspiel Maulbach", part 2, p. 9.

The day laborer Johannes Weber[6], in his mid-50s from Dannenrod, is also to be deported to the New World in 1871. This does not succeed: He should have gone to New York with the "Christel", but he returns home in 1872 and claims that the German Society of the City of New York, which takes care of newcomers, has sent him back. Nobody believes him. Did he even go on board in Bremerhaven?

Most of them have to pay for their passage themselves or go into debt bondage with Americans. Shipowners, agents, carters, outfitters, innkeepers, and hoteliers, all earn money from emigration. In the Vogelsberg and neighboring regions there are several contact points. Since 1828, the Storndorf freight driver Heinrich Rausch has been authorized to broker passages, as can be seen from his advertisement in a newspaper of February 1848: "Emigrants to North America can continually be transported on good solid three-masted first-class ships at the cheapest prices. In bringing this to the attention of the emigrants, I notice that for almost 20 years now I have been engaged in the transport of emigrants to North America to the greatest satisfaction of the emigrants and am therefore licensed as a certified agent and have provided an appropriate deposit. I take care of the transport from here to Bremen with my own wagon and horses, scheduled for the first and fifteenth of each month."[7]

---

[6] Seim, Auswanderung, part 2, p. 12
[7] Intelligenzblatt für den Kreis Alsfeld, Februar 1848.

And when we go on board, go on board,
and when we go on...
And when we go on board, go on board,
and when we go on board,
Ours will be the tweendeck, lower, lower tweendeck,
Ours will be the tweendeck, and we'll be lice's...
Ours will be the tweendeck, lower, lower tweendeck,
Ours will be the tweendeck,
and we'll be lice's port!

Expectations are high, and so is uncertainty. As early as 1830 they are singing in Germany:[*]

Oh, how many beautiful things
you hear from America.
That's where we want to go to,
that's where you have the most beautiful life.

Sometimes it so cold here, we could freeze to death,
and can hardly move our fingers.
And it is warm there even in winter.
Nobody gets poor buying wood.

The largest fish known,
you can catch it with your bare hand.
The carp are, on my honor,
often weighing half a hundred kilo.

The chocolate and sugar cane
grow at every pond.

---

[*] Amerika, folksong, 19th century, composer unknown, see the website of the Volksliederarchiv.

Gabriele Gonder Carey with her husband and her sons.

It is hard to believe:
Wool grows on every tree.

And when we came to the port,
we were pale with grief!
Everything we took with us,
we had to pay for the freight.

We went out to sea,
and many cried out, "Oh and woe!"
And the children look pathetic.
Oh, Father, oh, Mother, when are we home?

Over the decades, the journey becomes shorter and the crossing a little more comfortable. In March 1841, Bremen shipowners advertised in the Alsfelder newspaper: "Notification for emigrants to North America. The undersigned hereby inform the public that on the first and fifteenth days of each month, as hitherto, they will dispatch large and fast-sailing, copper-plated, three-masted German ships from Bremen equipped with high spacious false ceilings to Baltimore and New York and at the appointment of the Administrator of the Grand Ducal Hessian Postal Administrator, Mr. Philipp Bäppler in Schellnhausen, as their agent."[9]

In the spring of 1851, around 3000 people left via Bremen in one month. Over the course of time, more than four million people from Europe are expected to take this

---

[9] Alsfelder Zeitung, März 1841.

route, for different motives. Thus, Democratic lawmakers flee overseas as the gains of the March Revolution of 1848 are abolished. They will be called "48ers" in the United States. During the economic crisis from the Weimar Republic, unemployed people such Heinrich Geissler from Ober-Gleen, the 23-year-old ladies' and men's tailor will leave. He emigrated in 1922 and found work in Baltimore. His nephew Walter Ruppenthal, the son of the village midwife Marie Ruppenthal, née Geissler, told in an e-mail in 2014 how emigration came about and what happened afterwards: "The Geissler family already had relatives in Buffalo with whom they were in correspondence. This was mainly run by my mother. At that time, she also announced to the Americans that her brother was unemployed and let them know that he would now actually have time to put their clothes in order. More or less an empty phrase, the consequences of which could not be foreseen. The next letter from Buffalo was accompanied by passage booking to the United States. My mother was severely reprimanded by her parents for this. The family was turned upside down. But my uncle Henry thought that was quite good and took the opportunity. With the help of relatives, he rented a small apartment and from then on carried out sewing work of all kinds. Business was going well, and he soon was able to gratefully return the money for the crossing."[10]

He took his chance. Therefore, no one will call him an economic refugee. Some Germans, however, follow the waves of emigration with mixed feelings. The song "A

---

[10] Walter Ruppenthal, see Felsing, „Himmel un Höll".

Proud Ship" is published in 1925, when steamships have long been traveling between the continents.

A proud ship "

A proud ship slowly slides through the waves
and carry on our German brethren.
The Eastern wind is blowing, the white sails are swelling.
America is their destination.
To stand on deck like this,
to look homeward:
America, to distant colonies.

Do you see them moving across the great ocean?
That's where they're going! Who dares to ask:

Why do they leave their home country?

Poor Germany, can you bear it,
how your sons are so harshly banished?
Look here, you who want to make people happy!
Look here, you oppressors!
See your best workers fleeing!
Do you see them moving across the great ocean?

There they move on blue ocean waves.
Why do they look back wistfully?
Are they so badly treated at home,
that they are now seeking their fortune in a foreign Land?

" „Ein stolzes Schiff", song of emigrants, 19th century, the lyrics were written and published by Heinrich Schacht (1817-1863) in 1855 in his book „Bilder aus Hamburg's Volksleben", p. 131 f.

What they couldn't find here,
they try to find there.
They sail away from German soil
and then find their grave in a foreign country.

Walter Ruppenthal's uncle became an American but stayed in touch with his family in Hesse. "In 1926 he came to visit me to attend my baptism and to persuade his bride, who had stayed behind in Ober-Gleen, to come along", the nephew wrote. "As far as I know, she would probably have been willing to do so. Unfortunately, the parents' veto caused this project to fail. Some people said that only 'good-for-nothings' go to America. As a result, the engagement broke up. My uncle Henry then met his future wife Käthe, born in 1905, from Ernstroda at the German Club. Together they ran a ladies' tailor's shop, which probably went very well. In 1934 they bought a slightly larger house. Their son Herbert was born in 1930 and their daughter Betty in 1935. Both the parents and children have visited us several times in Germany. And, of course, we've been there several times."

Where there are Germans, Germans go. This also applies to emigrants from Upper Hesse: in 1927, the Jewish tailor Nathan Lamm[12] from Ober-Gleen goes to Buffalo, as well. He explains to the immigration authorities that he wants to go to Buffalo, where Heinrich Geissler lives. In the 1930 Census, he is listed as Max Nathan Lamm, as Amy B. Cohen, the author of the Brotmanblog, has found out. Nathan

---

[12] Nathan Lamm from Ober-Gleen is mentioned by Amy B. Cohen, the author of „Pacific Street" in her blog: https://brotmanblog.com/tag/lamm. More about family Lamm from Ober-Gleen on the Lamm pages on My Heritage, by Linda Silverman-Shefler.

worked in the United States, first as a baker, then in construction; was in the United States Army from 1942 and returned to Buffalo after the end of the war. In those years, opponents of the Nazis and those persecuted because of their Jewish origins desperately tried to get a visa for the United States. What happened to some of them we will learn later. Let's go back to the early 19th century, first.

It is not uncommon for many people to get rid of their money before they are leaving their homecountry. And so, in 1832, the Bremen Senate, concerned about the good reputation of the city, instructed the innkeepers "that everything that seems necessary for the benefit of those who have chosen Bremen as their place of emigration should be taken into account as much as possible". In order to protect people leaving Europe via Bremen, the first state law is passed in Germany in the same year: the "Ordinance on Emigrants with Local or Foreign Ships". From now on, passenger lists are mandatory and, from 1852, must be handed over to the "Verification Bureau for Emigrants", which was specially set up by the Chamber of Commerce.

If subjects want to leave Hesse-Darmstadt, they must first submit an application. The mayor forwards it to the Grand Ducal District Office in Alsfeld. The newspaper then calls on potential creditors to come forward within three months. More and more people are arriving in Bremen. The first way leads to the verification office. And they are looking for accommodations. Are there still rooms available in the hostel "The City of Baltimore" at the Neue

Markt? In the "City of New York" on Grosse Johannisstrasse or "Zum Admiral Nelson" on Langenstrasse? There are not enough rooms anymore. And so, businessman Friedrich Missler has emigration halls built in Bremen-Findorff. He offers an all-round service: lodging, tickets, insurance, information. Mostly via ships of the Norddeutsche Lloyd.

Those who are not allowed to leave, vanish: Young men who want to avoid military service are among them, such as Friedrich Trump from Kallstadt an der Weinstrasse, who will become rich as an innkeeper and brothel owner during the gold rush. Poachers also disappear without deregistering, debtors, sometimes even entire families, Social Revolutionaries who are wanted by the police, husbands who abandon their wives, young people and others who do not expect to get a permit. On 1 January 1848, a newspaper in Upper Hesse reports: "The Regional Court of the Grand Ducal Hessian of Homberg to the mayors of the district. In recent times, it has often been the case that persons have emigrated to America without first entrusting anyone in their former homeland with the care of their affairs, which then sometimes resulted in the ordering of costly judicial curates, but always the delay of inheritance disputes and similar transactions. We therefore call on you to draw the attention of the emigrants, in their own interest and the interest of their remaining relatives, to the disadvantages of failing to make such a power of attorney. Signed, G. Klingelhöffer."[13]

In Hesse-Kassel, emigration is no longer illegal from 1831 onwards. People have already left before, as it says on the

---

[13] Intelligenzblatt für den Kreis Alsfeld und die benachbarten Kreise, January 1, 1848.

pages of the Neustadt family research.[14] From 1820 to 1840 they gathered at the "burned oak" in the Wasenberg Forest to trek north. They need four to five days with their horse-drawn carriages for the first stage. In Hannoversch-Münden, horses and carts are sold. And the journey continues with Weser barges to Bremen and Bremerhaven, five to six days on the river. In 1852, the Main-Weser Railway is built, connecting Kassel and Frankfurt am Main. For many emigrants from the region, this shortens the journey by days. You take the train to Karlshafen and board a Weser steamship, then a sailing ship in Bremerhaven. In advertisements, passengers leave reviews after the crossing, whether paid or on their own initiative. In 1841, in the newspaper from Alsfeld the people read: "Thanks to Captain J. H. Bosse. The undersigned passengers of Mr. Friedrich Jacob Wichelhausen in Bremen feel compelled of their own accord to praise the excellent efficiency, untiring attention, activity and caution of the Captain, Mr. J. H. Bosse, of which they had the opportunity to convince themselves day and night, to boast publicly and both for this and for the courtesy shown to them, kindness, and humanity to express their warmest gratitude. With the frequent complaints about the carelessness of some captains, the happiness of getting into such philanthropic and sympathetic hands is doubly beneficial, and we can only hope that a similar thing will happen to our subsequent compatriots. New York, June 4, 1841, E. A.

---

[14] Information about emigration from Neustadt and the surrounding area on https://familienforschung-neustadt-hessen.de.

Schumann for himself and on behalf of the remaining 185 passengers."[15]

Why break up when you can stay together? In Neustadt in Kurhesse, some families decided to emigrate together in 1832, as can be read on the website about family research in Neustadt. The "Columbus", a three-masted ship of a Bremen shipping company is to bring the almost 200 people from Neustadt, Momberg and the region to America. At the end of May, the ship departs from Bremerhaven and reaches New York in mid-July, after a trip of six weeks. Around 1880, the emigrant song was sung in Upper Hesse:[16]

Now is the time and hour
to travel to America
The wagons are already at the door.
With wife and children we march.

The friends and our relatives
reach out to us for the last time:
"Friends, don't cry so much,
see you now and never!"

And when we arrived in Bremen
and looked at the big water.
We are not afraid of a waterfall:
God is everywhere.

---

[15] Alsfelder Zeitung, 1841.

[16] from Upper Hesse and Wetterau, 1880/90, see Volksliederarchiv.

And when we came to Baltimore,
we raised our hands
and exclaimed: Victoria!
Now we are in America.
We traveled even further away
and trusted in dear Lord,
The idleness is now over.
Brothers, we have to work!

At least 15,000 people from the old district of Alsfeld are said to have emigrated to the United States via Bremerhaven between 1825 and 1900, the majority of whom were day laborers and craftsmen. Families and single people have set off from Bremerhaven for New York, Philadelphia or Baltimore. Even though the meals on the German ships are supposed to be much better than in earlier times, the German Society of the City of New York still recommends in 1883 that those wishing to leave the country take provisions with them:[17] "Smoked ham and lean meat sausage, even a piece of good cheese that lasts, is best suited for this. Zweiback and a few oranges or lemons will prove to be a very welcome addition along the way. Drinks will be purchased on board all German steamers at cheap prices, condensed milk for the children will be administered free of charge. The following applies to meals on the tweendeck: It is served for breakfast: coffee with milk and sugar, white bread, and rye bread with butter. Lunch at 12 o'clock: soup with vegetables in

---

[17] Rathgeber für Auswanderungswillige, "Practical Advice and Information for Emigrants", mentioned in the Annual Report of the German Society of the City of New York of 1883. Also for the following quotations, concerning the recommendations of the German Society of the City of New York.

it, meat, and potatoes. In the afternoon at 3 o'clock: coffee with milk and sugar. In the evening at 7 o'clock: tea or coffee with milk and sugar, white bread, and rye bread with butter."

If you travel in the tweendeck, you should buy a straw sack and tin dishes, preferably in the harbor, the German Society also advises in 1883. Warm clothes and blankets are important, diapers and wipes for the toddlers, but otherwise only the essentials, packed in sturdy, lockable, not too large boxes, because it is often stolen on board, and the passengers with the cheap tickets have to carry their luggage themselves. Smoking is prohibited on the tween deck. Matches, gunpowder and other flammable objects, rifles and other weapons shall be handed over to the master for safekeeping. Gambling is prohibited. And if the officer on duty orders it, the tween deck must be tidied up or scrubbed. Twice a day, a doctor comes by to check on the passengers. It is necessary to prevent the smallpox or other diseases from spreading, by vaccination for example, as the German Society of the City of New York writes.

The ship's doctors shall vaccinate those who have not yet been vaccinated and issue to them a health certificate, which the immigrants shall keep to show to the medical officer upon arrival at the port of destination. To isolate the immigrants affected by smallpox at sea, and their luggage is to be properly disinfected.

Paying attention to cleanliness, not entrusting anything personal to ship acquaintances, patiently enduring seasickness, these are also advice for the trip. And in Castle Garden in New York, a station that passengers have to pass through from the intermediate deck, members of the German Society are on hand to assist the newcomers. If you can read, you can recognize them by the inscription on their caps. In the emigrant novel "Jürnjakob Swehn, der Amerikafahrer" by Johannes Gillhoff,[18] the first-person narrator, a Mecklenburger, asks: "How smart do you think someone is when they come across? As stupid as the piglet of a day laborer, one like the other. If stupidity hurt, there would be nothing to hear at New York Harbor from morning to evening but howling and lamentation. But that soon becomes unlearned. One is also pushed around here in a completely different way than over there, and if you are only a few times properly offended with one's thick head, then you soon learn to be careful and stand firmly on your feet and grasp firmly. If you can't do that, you should save the travel money and should not look at Germany with your back. Because there, the good God is still guardian of the stupid. That doesn't really apply here. This is where most of them have their dear God in their money box. I could tell funny stories about some of those who came across. But I don't want to reprimand anyone, and most of them would only have my own image."

Some come to America in a roundabout way. In Ober-Gleen, the descendants of linen weaver Michael Schott holds the record. The genealogist Carolyn Schott from Seattle, author of the guidebook "Visiting your Ancestral Town", has followed the traces of her family, from early

---

[18] Gillhoff, Jürnjakob Swehn, der Amerikafahrer.

18th century when Michael left his homevillage until the emigration of his descendants to the United States in 1905. "My family roots are in Ober-Gleen", Carolyn Schott says. "My great-great-great-great-great grandfather Michael Schott was born in Ober-Gleen in the late sixteen hundreds, and so that is where my family originated in Germany. You know, when I was growing up, I always knew my family was German. My parents spoke German, we ate German foods. Being German was a very big part of who I was growing up. And so, it was something to explore and to understand more about. My five times grandfather Michael, when he left Ober-Gleen, first he moved to Osthofen, a town on the Rhine River, right by the Rhine River. And a couple of generations later, his grandson left Osthofen and went to Emperial Russia and settled in a village that is currently Moldowia, but then the family moved to a couple of German villages in the Ukraine. (...) So they lived in Ukraine for several generations but maintaining their German heritage. And then my grandfather left Ukraine and came to the United States."[19]

The Gonder family also took a little longer to emigrate to the United States. Two generations, to be exact. Around 1890, the tailor Georg Gonder from Ober-Gleen settled in Hamburg instead of emigrating like his older brother Ludwig. So, his children had what many Germans wished for in bad times: an "uncle in America". Georg's great-granddaughter Gabriele Gonder-Carey, an archivist, did some research and found out that Ludwig who called

---

[19] See publications of Lastoria e.V., written by Monika Felsing, like "Himmel un Höll" and the audio cds that come along with the books. And the book and the website of Carolyn Schott, with her blog.

himself Louis in the United States, bought land in Washington State and had a large farm. Gabriele has been told that he was called "Hop King of Washington" but isn't sure if that's true.[20]

Hops and the beer that was made of it was something German immigrants were famous for, as producers and as consumers. A Bavarian, John Wagner, who settled in Philadelphia is taken for the pioneer of lager in the United States, but around 1840, other immigrants were also already producing their own beer, and more and more followed. Over the decades, brewers from Bavaria, but also from Bremen, Lower Saxony and Hamburg succeeded on the American market. Today, in the century of craft beer, you can drink "Hessian Horseman" or "Angry Hessian" in the United States, not to mention "Headless Hessian Pumpkin Ale". But that's a completely different story.

Georg Gonder from Ober-Gleen in Upper Hesse started a family in Altona. His great-granddaughter assumes that the family has Huguenot roots. Also because of the brown eyes. In the 17th century, French Protestants fled to Hesse, and several thousand to Hesse-Kassel. The refugees brought with them a few of the fairy tales that Dorothea Viehmann told the brothers Grimm much later. Once upon a time...

But now let's fast forward to the 20th century. One of Georg Gonder's grandsons has involuntarily spent several years in France – as a prisoner of war after the Second

---

[20] Informations about family Gonder are from emails and have been published by Lastoria in books about Ober-Gleen, written by Monika Felsing.

Changed his mind in Hamburg: Georg Gonder from Ober-Gleen.

World War. In 1947 Uwe Gonder returned to Hamburg and married a Swabian. This brings us to the next generation: Gabriele, born in 1954, who migrated as a child. Her father and her mother and the seven-year-old girl went to Southern California in 1961, where Gabriele's mother had an aunt and uncle. Her father told her that he had wanted a change. There were probably also economic reasons for emigrating, as Gabriele thinks, but these were not the most important reasons. Her father's uncle had found a job for him. Uwe Gonder worked as a toolmaker at Mattel for 20 years. And Gabriele had a lot of Barbies...

For anyone who does family history research and has ancestors who emigrated, passenger lists are important sources which are now easily accessible. And so it is clear: People from Upper Hesse have also been drawn to Canada. In the 1860s, Johannes Heinrich Diegel,[21] born in 1816 in Ober-Gleen, and his wife Katharine, née Vollgert from Ehringshausen, went to Canada. Their great-great-grandson, Lutheran pastor Matthew Hartmann Diegel, born in 1960, lives in Errington Township, Ontario, like many people with roots in the former Grand Duchy of Hesse-Darmstadt. His father was born in 1933 in Brodhagen, Logan Township, in the same village as his grandfather in 1900 and great-grandfather in 1873.

Heinrich Lemcke's Canada Guide from 1896 was definitely not needed by the third-generation Canadian. For others it might have been helpful, especially the ten "Golden Rules for Emigrants":[22]

---

[21] Information about family Diegel by Matthew Diegel, Canada. The family is mentioned in the books of Lastoria about Ober-Gleen, written by Monika Felsing.

1. "First think about it, then start it."
2. "To act first and to think about it afterwards has already brought a lot of suffering to some."
3. "Never trust anyone's word."
4. "Never sign a document whose contents you do not know."
5. "Never use a hack lawyer."
6. "Never sign contracts in a foreign language without being well informed of their content by reliable and noninvolved people."
7. "Never buy land without first inspecting it closely."
8. "Never buy more than you can pay."
9. "Over there, always stick to the societies of your homeland, which have been established for the protection of immigrants. If you've become wealthy over there, support these clubs and be grateful, it's a matter of honor for you."
10. "Interest must bear your wealth, not only earthly, but also in higher and better goods."

First think about it, then start it. Or let it be. Those who do not want to emigrate hope for better times. In 1874, Georg Fett from Maulbach in Upper Hesse assured his brother-in-law Wilhelm Sommer, who lived in Indiana, that the economy was going uphill. The Malter wheat now costs 16 to 17 guilders, grain 12, barley 10, the pound of butter 30, the pound of meat 21 guilders. And with prices, wages have risen. "A proper servant now gets the year 150, also 175 guilders. We have heard that it would be a bad time in America right now because many people go around unemployed, and many even come back to

---

[22] Heinrich Lemcke, epilogue of the Guide to Canada, Kanadaführer.

Germany. Your cousin Heinrich Engel von Obergleen sends you his best regards."[23]

Catharina Büttner, née Lanz from Maulbach, writes to her parents in 1859 together with her husband Konrad from Illinois: "Dear Father, you write that you have been thinking about us for many days. Dear old father, I wish that all your children had like me. I have it three times better here than in Germany. In Germany, the poor people don't have potatoes to eat yet, much less anything else, but that's not the case here. If a man creates here, he can eat whatever he wants. You don't have to give everything to the landgrave here like in Germany. What would we have in Germany, maybe a cow or guilt and impatience. We don't need to push cows here. We now have four beautiful horses, four cows, 20 pigs, 2 to 3 hundred chickens. This year we will slaughter 6 pigs that are bigger than the one you slaughtered from time to time. I eat more eggs and butter in a week than you in Germany in a year. If a man works hard here, he can build up an existence, but not in Germany. If you are poor, you will stay poor."[24]

Catharina would like to have her siblings with her, so she tries to reassure her parents and is more worried about her brother Andreas, as a conscript, will no longer be allowed to leave the country. The signs in Europe point to war, which will begin in 1866 and which the Hessians, as allies of the Austrians, will lose to the Prussians. This is followed by the German-French War of 1870-71 and the

---

[23] Seim, Auswanderung, part 2, p. 58 f.
[24] Seim, Auswanderung, part 2, p. 55 f.

Genealogist Carolyne Schott (left) and the author in Upper Hesse.

The first two generations of U.S. citizens of family Schott.

founding of the German Empire. "I have heard again in the newspaper that the King of Prussia, with whom we have got along here, is not to be feared by next spring. This is what the newspaper writes in Germany. You think we have war here as well as in Germany. The war here is nothing, I don't need to be afraid of that. They want to drive the Indians away, that's all the war here. I dream of my brother Andreas, he should have given a lot of thought to the soldier's life, so be so good and write me how it goes on."

From 1861 to 1865, the American Civil War raged, in which many Germans also participated. From 1860 to 1880, the massacre of 350 peaceful men, women and children at Wounded Knee, the white settlers and the U.S. Army also persecuted the indigenous people incessantly. Their number drops from four million to 250,000, and they do not receive civil rights until 1924. What people in Hesse or Bremen knew about Indians and the Wild West in the 19th century came from letters and newspapers, from novels by James Fenimore Cooper and Karl May, from the books of the Hamburg adventurer Friedrich Gerstäcker or from the Wild West show by Buffalo Bill Cody, which also stopped at the velocipede racecourse in Bremen and in the Palmengarden of Frankfurt/Main in 1890. In 1848, Georg Treu published a practical "Guide for emigrants, agents, businessmen who come into contact with the emigration system" in Bamberg. The book contains, among other things, a collection of the "most important decrees and diplomatic documents published in the southern German states, Bremen and North America" and a brief description of the United States. The author recommends Bremen as the "first and most excellent embarkation place".

It is ensured there by laws that the emigrants are not only protected from overreaching, but also that they are well fed and treated on the ships.[25]

And Treu warns those who want to emigrate that they should not have illusions: "Whoever lacks activity, diligence and perseverance, who shies away from privation, work and effort, let him stay at home, because he will achieve something even less on the other side of the sea than on this side. Many who dreamed of golden mountains here have lost their own beyond and have degenerated into poverty and misery or returned here as beggars. (...) Romancers and so-called do-gooders will always be deceived in the most delicate way by the bare reality of their reveries and ideas. There is no field of activity for such people in America, nor is there much to hope for scholars, lawyers, theologians, pharmacists, and servants, and they are usually compelled to earn their living by hard, unaccustomed work. Even for doctors, the prospects are by no means bright, since the number of existing ones, already very large almost everywhere and quackery plays an extensive role. The best accommodation is found by people from the day labourers, peasants and craftsmen's classes."[26]

And which trades are particularly in demand? Beer brewer, distiller, tailor, shoemaker, milliner, furrier, glove maker, beutler, tanner, butcher, baker, confectioner,

---

[25] Treu, S. 112.
[26] Treu, S. 109 ff.

watchmaker, bricklayer, carpenter, blacksmith, coppersmith, nail smith, plumber, wainwright, varnisher, saddler, trimmer, brick burner, miller, book printer, bookbinder, pewter founder, cooper, stuff printer.[27]

Conrad Felsing from Ober-Gleen in today's Vogelsberg district, as a master carpenter, also sees good opportunities for himself in America, although he can't write. In his mid-thirties, he sailed from Hamburg to New York in 1836 with the "Howard", without his wife Anna Maria and without his children. And that, like the emigration port of Hamburg, is unusual for Upper Hesse. The authorities do not like it when family fathers disappear from the scene, because the community has to care for the wife and the children, then.

As much as the family knows, it took Anna Maria a long time to make her way from northern Germany to Hesse with three small children and without money. Everything she and her husband had owned, they sold before they left. Anna Maria will be dependent on her creditors and relatives for the rest of her life. All that awaited her was the grave of her eldest son. He had died in 1835 at the age of about six and had been buried by Pastor Friedrich Ludwig Weidig. Shortly thereafter, Weidig is arrested in the Ober-Gleen rectory and jailed in Darmstadt prison. His wife Amalie hopes in vain for his release. Anna Maria Felsing will also never see her husband again. He's gone, lost in America. As if he had never existed. Later research in archives and databases comes to nothing.

---

[27] Treu, S. III.

Our Conrad lies over the ocean [28]

Our Conrad lies over the ocean,
our Conrad lies over the sea.
Our Conrad lies over the ocean,
oh, bring back our Conrad to me!

Bring back, bring back,
oh, bring back our Conrad to me, to me,
bring back, bring back,
oh, bring back our Conrad to me!

His wife Anna and his dear children,
oh, they stood alone at the pier.
Didn't they have money for tickets?
Or why, or why they are still here?

Bring back, bring back,
oh, bring back our Conrad to me, to me,
bring back, bring back,
oh, bring back our Conrad to me!

From farm to farm did she go back,
worked for bed and also for bread,
in Hesse she started with nothing
and believed her husband was dead.

Bring back, bring back,
oh, bring back our Conrad to me, to me,

[28] Coversong to the melody of the folksong „My Bonnie Lies Over the Ocean", lyrics by Monika Felsing about her ancestors Conrad and Anna Maria Felsing, based on research by genealogist Matthias Eislöffel, Frankfurt/Main.

bring back, bring back,
oh, bring back our Conrad to me!

Nobody has found out what happened,
only that he had reached the port.
Without any trace, Conrad vanished.
And Anna, she prayed to the Lord.

Bring back, bring back,
oh, bring back our Conrad to me, to me,
bring back, bring back,
oh, bring back our Conrad to me!

He never wrote her a letter,
our carpenter, he couldn't write.
Anna's life never got better,
no widow, no one at her side.

Bring back, bring back,
oh, bring back my Conrad to me, to me,
bring back, bring back,
oh, bring back my Conrad to me!

One day, she gave birth to a daughter,
no father officially known.
Her eldest son died when he was six.
this is what the church books have shown.
Conrad, Conrad,
why did you leave them all alone, alone?
Conrad, Conrad,
why didn't you ever come home?

Where to go in America? In 1848, Georg Treu recommended settling in one of the western states, although not on the west coast: in Ohio, Indiana, Missouri, Pennsylvania, Michigan, Illinois or Wisconsin. States which, in his estimation, have a climate very similar to that in Germany, and in which the prices of land are not yet too high. He gives tips on currency exchange, insurance, citizenship and buying land, and warns against thieves and fraudsters. So, he advises every newcomer, "that he should be careful when leaving the ship, that he should carry his cash with him wherever possible, and that he should not let anyone know that he had anything. He should not trust anyone who approaches him to give him his good advice, even if this person speaks German and makes him the most beautiful promises in terms of employment, land purchase, travel opportunity, housing and the like."[29]

Germans should also be wary of Americans in general, Georg Treu warns his compatriots. "As a rule, the American is clever, very skillful in life and business, sharp-sighted, active, inquisitive and extremely addicted to money and profit. For the German, and especially for the new immigrant, extreme caution is therefore necessary if he does not want to see himself deceived and betrayed at every step. He cannot be suspicious enough in this regard. In addition, the American is proud and considers his nation the first in the world. The Germans are not held in high esteem by him, and they are usually given the derisive name dutchmen."[30]

[29] Treu, p. 117 ff.
[30] Treu, p. 125.

Aaron Marx from Sterbfritz in the Union Army in 1862.

Mildred Marx, a granddaughter of Aaron and Brünel Marx nee Lamm.

Who were whose ancestors and where did they go? Not many genealogists are as active as Linda Silverman Shefler, a descendant of Brünel Lamm from Ober-Gleen. Her family had been living in this little village in Upper Hesse for at least 200 years, from 18th Century until the Nazi time. Linda Silverman Shefler shares the results of several decades of research, several ten thousands of names and a lot of life stories, on MyHeritage.

"I am the second great granddaughter of Bertha Lamm, who was born in Ober-Gleen in 1832", she says. "I knew a lot about Bertha's husband, Aaron Marx who was from Sterbfritz, and even grew up with a picture of him, taken when he served in the Union Army during the American Civil War. But Bertha remained a mystery. Thirty years ago, when I started my family research, the wife of a second cousin of my grandmother told me the only thing she knew about 'Grandma Bertha' was that Bertha had family in Baltimore, Maryland. It took me twenty years before I was finally able to figure out who Bertha's family was and where she was originally from. From my research, I've been able to figure out some of the details of her life. Bertha was born Brünel Lamm in February 1832. She was the daughter of Jacob Eleaser Lösmann, who took the surname Lamm in January 1809, and his wife, Süss Höchster, from Storndorf. She was the fifth of eight children. There were four boys and four girls. It was quite common in the 1800s for Jewish girls to leave their families and immigrate to America. The primary reason was that their parents couldn't afford the dowry, the aussteuer, for more than one or two daughters, and in America a dowry wasn't necessary. Many times, girls would

Henry Geissler with his family in Buffalo.

travel in groups of cousins, or groups from the same village, and they would settle in cities where there was a large community of German Jews. I have never found the ship manifest for Bertha, but I suspect she came to America with cousins from her mother's Höchster family, as many of them also immigrated in the 1850s. Bertha was the only one of her siblings to emigrate, as a matter-of-fact, no one else from her family (that I could find) came to America, until the children of her brother settled in Baltimore in the 1880s."

Baltimore was one of the favoured destinations for Upper Hessians in the United States. But where did Bertha go? "Bertha settled initially in Cincinnati, Ohio, where she met and married my second great-grandfather Aaron Marx in 1856", Linda Silverman-Shefler has found out. "After Cincinnati they spent some years in a town outside of Cleveland where Aaron worked as a bookbinder. Some-time in 1861 they moved to Erie, Pennsylvania, where Aaron joined the Union Army. They stayed there until 1869, when they moved to Cleveland. By then, Bertha was the mother of six sons and one daughter, born in four different cities. I believe they moved to Cleveland as Bertha had a lot of relatives there from the Höxter family. Aaron went on to become the first Jewish policeman of Cleveland in 1870 and he remained on the police force until his retirement in January 1897 at the age of 63. Sadly, Bertha died shortly after Aaron retired, in August of 1897, at the age of 65."[31]

---

[31] Linda Silverman-Shefler's statements, audios, have been quoted in „Himmel un Höll", a book about Ober-Gleen, written by Monika Felsing, are on the cd that comes with the book and in the audio book „Yiddish Life". On My Heritage, Linda Silverman-Shefler is responsible for the pages about family Lamm from Ober-Gleen and for pages about her ancestors from Storndorf, Kirtorf, Diez upon Lahn, Sterbfritz and many other places. A precious source for genealogists.

Henry Geissler and his wife as tourists in Germany in 1954.

Amazingly for the 19th Century, all of Bertha's seven children survived childhood and lived long lives. Today there are six generations of descendants of Bertha and Aaron. But not every Hessian migrant has founded a family in America. During the time of the gold rush, young girls and women from Hesse go to the Wild West as Hurdy Gurdy Girls, sell dances for a dollar and prostitute themselves. In 1864, four 15- to 17-year-olds from the Butzbach area follow a man who wanted to bring them to California as barrel organ players. He has promised them a thousand guilders a year, twenty times as much as a maid or seamstress earns annually. When the girls are picked up in Düsseldorf, they don't even have papers with them. Jewish women from Galicia are among the preferred victims of the matchmakers. In 1902, Rabbi Leopold Rosenak from Bremen publicly warns against such "traffickers for girls"[32], and the League of Nations tries to fight "white slavery". Brothels were waiting for many young women, if not factories or fields. A Klezmer song from the early 20th Century played by Burghard Bock, Bremen, that is included in the podcast tells the sad story of a beautiful, cheerful Jewish immigrant whose American dream hasn't come true: the green cousin.[33]

Freedom is a precious commodity in America – not for the natives, the Asian railroad workers, or the black slaves, but for most of the whites. Especially for the men among them. Georg Treu comments: "What has my greatest applause of the vaunted American freedom, says Vulpius,

---

[32] Die Gartenlaube, no. 25, 1889, p. 1, „Rettung vor Seelenhandel".

[33] Burghard Bock (Mandriola), "Di grine Kuzine", live-recording during his concert at the history workshop „Deutschland auf der Flucht. Exil in Amsterdam 1933-1945" (Germany on the Run. Exile in Amsterdam 1933-1945) in the Villa Ichon in May 2022.

is that the individual in the United States, according to his inner urge and circumstances, can move freely on the outside. He can come and go when and where he wants. If he doesn't like it in one place, he packs up and wanders someplace else, without being attacked by gensdarmes and policemen and asked for his passport, nor inhibited by guild institutions or similar stories. Incidentally, this freedom also has its dark side, among other things, that everywhere, depending on the size of a place, one finds a lot of unemployed people who cannot find work, or day thieves and loafers who do not want to find one, who now stay in the boarding houses and taverns and make their living with card games and all sorts of other finger arts."[34]

And unlike in Germany, there is freedom of trade, only lawyers need an exam, neither doctors nor teachers nor clergy. If you want, you can try your hand at all kinds of professions, even several at the same time. Congregations can hire and dismiss their pastors and teachers themselves. And it is not only the question of dowry or trousseau that plays a lesser role in the surplus of men in the United States, which is why immigrant women often find a man quite quickly, not infrequently one with a similar origin. And the best news for all those who are as poor as church mice and are not allowed to decide for themselves: In America, couples do not need the approval of a local council to get married. "If a couple wants to get married, all it takes that they go to the pastor or justice of the peace and make their declaration. From the latter, it then receives a confirmation slip, which costs two dollars, five guilders. That's the end of it."[35]

---

[34] Treu, pp. 125 ff

In his travel guide Georg Treu also explains the form of government – and thus democracy. This is uncharted territory for Germans who will not live in a republic until after the First World War. "North America has no emperors, kings, princes, but every four years the people elect a man from among themselves, to whom the highest dignity in the country is conferred. This man's title is the President. When the time of his administration is over, he descends again from his height and becomes, as before, a simple citizen. The President can be elected for a second time, but not for the third time, he receives an annual salary of 25,000 dollars or 60,000 guilders because of his office, certainly a very insignificant sum compared to European conditions. Each individual state is independent, has its own representation of the people, orders its internal administration independently of the federal government and enacts its own laws."[36]

For example, on the abolition of slavery in Missouri, with active Hessian participation, as we will hear in the next part. Some suffered from homesickness forever, and others, like Friedrich Münch from Nieder-Gemünden, Herbert Sondheim from Ober-Gleen, Ruth Stern Gasten from Nieder-Ohmen, or Ruth Stern Glass Ernest from Dietz, returned to their birthplace once, but didn't feel at home anymore. In the podcast, a coversong of "Waltzing Matilda" is heard, with lyrics written by Monika Felsing from Ober-Gleen is about that feeling of alienation. It had been recorded spontaneously in 2018, together with the audience in the former Synagogue of

---

[35] Treu, pp. 125 ff.

[36] Treu, p. 129.

Ober-Gleen in Upper Hessian dialect. "Go away, come back, even you won't stay here", the refrain says. "What binds you to a place are the people, also those who aren't alive anymore. Nature is vulnerable, houses can be destroyed, and it would be a lie to say it doesn't matter. Your soul sings a song of past times. You know that clocks stand still if they are not wound up or out of order, but time never sleeps. Go away, come back. Something of you will stay here."

Departure to freedom

Of 500 who set out to find and fight for human rights. Some of them have changed the country they settled in, for the better

Brüder, so kann's nicht gehn [1]

Brothers, it can't go like this.
Let's stand together!
Don't tolerate it anymore!
Freedom, your tree's rotting,
everyone's at the begging stick
and will soon die of hunger.
People to the gun!
Brothers in gold and silk,
brother in peasant dress,
reach out to each other!
Germany's distress calls you all,
as does Lord's commandment:
Kill your tormentors,
save the country!
Kill your tormentors,
save the country!

Revolutionary Upper Hesse. To the melody of "God save the King", Karl Follen has written the lyrics of a freedom song. Karl was born in Romrod, Upper Hesse in 1796, the

---

[1] Karl Follen 1825, as performed by Duo Eigenart from Nidderau/Hesse at the Weidig weekend in Ober-Gleen, 2015. An orbituary is in Friedrich Münch, Gesammelte Schriften, p. 38.

son of the Giessen lawyer Christoph Follenius and his wife Rosine. The radical democrat has to leave the country. In 1824, when he is to be arrested in Switzerland, he flees to America. His younger brother, the lawyer Paul Follenius from Giessen, and Paul's brother-in-law, the pastor Friedrich Münch from Nieder-Gemünden, spread a "request and declaration regarding a large-scale emigration from Germany to the North American Free States". Their note becomes the cornerstone of the Giessen Emigration Society. Follenius and Münch want to live in freedom on American soil, together with like-minded Germans who can afford a fresh start: "We intend to unite all German emigrants into one large society, so that all grow in one and the same area", they wrote. "Where we Germans can remain with German language and customs, where we can make our institutions ourselves by mutual agreement, support each other in the strongest possible way and lead a free, peaceful and happy life under the protection of the government of the Free States." This would be possible "if all German emigrants settle in the same region, until, with the help of later and gradual growth of compatriots from the old homeland, also from individual states of the Union itself, a German Free State, a rejuvenated Germany in North America, can be formed and German nationality can acquire a respected voice in the League of Nations"[2].

Looking back, Friedrich Münch will write: "The first colonies were to be joined by new ones every year until

---

[2] Follenius/Münch, Aufforderung, p. 5. More about the people from Nieder-Gemünden, Lich, Otterbach, Rohrbach, Rodheim, Erbenheim, Babenhausen, Stammheim, Büdingen, Bohbach, Sachsen, Württemberg, Thüringen, Bayern, Hannover, Hamburg, Böhmen and Preußen on board of the „Medora": „Utopia" and https://sommer-republik.de.

the necessary population was available to enter a new state into the Union. Since we were only too well aware of the political and social infirmities that had been fought in vain in the old world for so long, and since in the new world everything had to be done all over again, even if only innocent and liberal people were to be accepted into society, we hoped, albeit on a smaller scale, to establish a model German republic from which a beneficial repercussion could be expected even on the old fatherland."[3] They were "not merely counting on the participation of those who were already accustomed to harder work as farmers and craftsmen": "It is precisely the participation of the educated that is indispensable in order to ensure the necessary measure of intellectual training for the whole for now and for all future."[4]

The revolutionary Friedrich Ludwig Weidig, a very popular scholar, rector from Butzbach, who is well connected throughout Europe and constantly monitored by the authorities, is to join them. But Weidig refuses. A serious dispute ensues. In the view of Friedrich Ludwig Weidig, it is a betrayal of the social revolution, even of the fatherland, to leave when you are needed most. The members of the Giessen Emigration Society, however, see no future for themselves and their children in the Grand Duchy of Hesse-Darmstadt. Münch and Follenius point out that they leave their homeland rather for political then for economical reasons: "It is obvious that this enterprise, if it is not to disintegrate, can only be started by those who are at least so well-off that, apart from the

[3] Münch, Friedrich, Gesammelte Schriften, p. 99.

[4] Aufforderung, p. 9.

costs of the passage, they have sufficient assets to be able to buy in North America as landowners or undertake any other trade. It is also clear that only respectful and hard-working families, who are no snobs, can be accepted into our society."[5]

The German Pioneer Association of Cincinnati, Ohio, published 1876 poems by Münch, also one from April 1834, which he wrote as a "farewell of the old world":[6]

Changeful human life!
Who'd bear his fate,
if there was no hope?
Hope shows us, to rise the soul,
peace and happiness
in the distance.
May time fly by,
Hope shall revive the heart
until the last moment!

What did the politician Carl Schurz say, who participated in the March Revolution of 1848 and fled to the United States with his wife Margarethe four years later? "Ideals are like stars. You will not succeed in touching them with your hand. But like the seafaring man on the desert of waters, you choose them as your guides, and following them you will reach your destiny."[7]

---

[5] Aufforderung, p. 9.
[6] Der deutsche Pionier, p.9.
[7] Carl Schurz, Faneuil Hall, Boston, April 18, 1859, as quoted on www.carl-schurz-haus.de. Carl Schurz who is also quoted on Muench related websites had been born in 1829 in Liblar, not far from Cologne, while his wife Margarethe Schurz nee Meyer came from a very rich family in Hamburg. Inspired by her elder sister Bertha (Baba) Ronge, she founded the first kindergarten in the U.S. with a concept acoording to Fröbel (see Hoerder, p. 62). Margarethe died in 1876 at the age of 43. A seventh child had been

The poet Hoffmann von Fallersleben who wrote the lyrics of the German national anthem, spent a lot of time in exile as a champion of democracy, but did not choose the path across the Atlantic. "My temporary Texas is called Holdorf," he once said. He saw friends and acquaintances moving far away and wrote a song about them in 1844, which can be heard on the CD "Die Schiffe nach Amerika" ("The Ships to America") by the band "Grenzgänger". Set to music by the Bremen musician Michael Zachcial. "Brothers, let's be glad," it says. Subtitle: "Here at the Mississipi"[8].

Brothers, let us raise our glasses merrily,
because we can live in freedom only abroad:
Can walk anywhere without a passport,
meet daily, without being harrassed by the police,
Here at the banks of the Mississippi.

Neither free thinking nor free speech
is taken here for a crime against state.
No policeman ever troubles us here,
and no one throws us into prison.
Here at banks of the Mississippi.

Titles, ranks and social classes

_____

born in England. The pioneer of kindergarten died in 1863, at the age of almost 45 in Frankfurt/Main. More about Berha on https://www.nifbe.de. Carl Schurz died in 1906. On the website of the Muench Family Association there is a short biography of „perhaps the most celebrated German-American of the 19th Century" who „as a fellow revolutionary for democracy" became „a good friend and political ally of the Muenches" and visited Georg Muench in Augusta in 1867. And the politician, attorney and author is quoted on the website: „If you want to be free there is but one way; it is to guarantee an equally full measure of liberty to all your neighbors."
[8] see https://www.von-fallersleben.de.

and such stupid stuff comes to an end here.
No priest may ever plague us here with hell,
No Jesuit will ever chase away our peace.
Here at the banks of the Mississippi.

In the past, we lived only as a punishment, as it were,
and they sheared us like sheep.
Brothers, let us sing, drink, dance!
No one has the right to tell us what to do here,
here at the banks of the Mississippi.

German Michel, don't continue to grow your seeds
for the army of civil servants and for the soldiers!
Michel, take heart to finally emigrate:
Here you belong to yourself, there only always to the
others,
Here at the banks of the Mississippi.

The interest in the emigration society is so great that they soon have to close the list. Passages for 500 people are ordered from the Bremen-based shipping company Everhard and Frederik Delius. On October 31, 1831, the first half travels with Follenius on the "Olbers" via New Orleans. Münch leads the second group and is haunted by bad luck. The ship they want to take does not come. A second one is also cancelled. And so the emigrants from Giessen are waiting on the Weser island of Harriersand near Brake for things to continue. They have to share four rooms, a kitchen, a cow and a horse stable and sleep in the hayloft. In July 1834, those who still wanted to be there finally took the "Medora" to Baltimore. The passenger list includes adults and minors from Thuringia, Coburg and Hesse, among others, including about 30 farmers, about ten academics and about 50 craftsmen, six maids, some women without a profession and about 50 children, including Münch's seven-year-old daughter Pauline and his six-year-old son Adolf, the children of his late wife Marianne Münch, née Borberg. One of the babies on board also belongs to the Münch family: it is the child of Friedrich's second wife Louise Münch, née Fritz.

How did they fare upon arrival? The bookseller Cornelius Schubert, a 21-year-old from Dessau, keeps a diary. "The first person who confronted us from the New World was the collector of the poll tax, which every immigrant has to pay with one and a half dollars and which is used to maintain a hospital for sick immigrants", he writes. "After this collector had left us, the doctor appeared, who examined the health status of all travelers. The heat was unbearable and had to be all the more so for us as we had to endure so much cold just before."[9]

Captain Griffith is in no hurry. He doesn't want to have his passengers' luggage brought ashore until the next morning. So the emigrants themselves lend a hand and carry the boxes off board. Baltimore's tax collectors are already waiting, as Cornelius Schubert describes it: "All things that are now good for one's own use are tax-free, including cloth and linen, books and everything that promotes the arts and sciences. After an eight-day stay in this really beautiful city, I rented a freight wagon together with two families. We loaded our luggage onto

---

° Rohrbach, M10b.

Washing machine from the 19th century in the
museum of Homberg/Efze.

it and drove out of the city. Two women, a maid and 6 children, all under 7 years of age, were on the wagon. We men walked in front, behind and next to the wagon in order to be able to reach up the often falling trifles again. I'm loaded with a double-barreled shotgun, a deer catcher and a hunting bag."[10]

The freight wagons take two weeks across the Alleghanny Mountains. The steamboat journey on the Ohio and Mississippi rivers to St. Louis takes another two weeks. The journey was exhausting, especially for the youngest, as Friedrich Münch later recalls: "The children suffered from tormenting skin rashes and I had to bury my youngest child after arrival, who gradually succumbed to the pernicious climatic influences."[11]

The Giessen Emigration Society has gradually dissolved. The Münch family settled near Dutzow in Warren County, in a hilly landscape on the Missouri, not far from Paul Follenius and Gottfried Duden's farm. The lawyer and former justice of the peace from Remscheid travelled to America as early as 1824 and campaigned massively for emigration after his return. His book "Report on a Journey to the Western States of North America and a Stay of Several Years on the Missouri River in the Years 1824 to 1827" made many of his compatriots dream of a better life. From a land of milk and honey overseas with apple, pear and cherry trees, wild vines and hunting grounds that do not belong to any nobleman. If you have a rifle,

---

[10] Rohrbach, MIIa.
[11] Rohrbach, MIIa.

you can go hunting, kill deer, turkeys, field chickens, pigeons, pheasants or snipes.

"One will not and cannot believe it in Europe how easy and pleasant it is to live in this country. It sounds too strange, too fabulous", Gottfried Duden wrote. "The belief in similar places on earth had long been banished to the fairy tale world. The inhabitants of the Mississippi counties, on the other hand, considered the reports of the hardship in Europe to be exaggerated. That there are so many white people there, who, with the greatest effort, hardly enjoy so much meat in a whole year as people feed to dogs here in a few weeks, that some families, without the mild donations of others, would even starve to death or freeze to death in winter, the citizens of the Missouri state, including their slaves, doubt so much, that they are accustomed to relate such statements only to the intention of flattering praise of America."[12]

The Giessen Emigration Society has sought advice from Duden, what Friedrich Münch regrets in retrospect: "According to the descriptions given by Duden, we had thought of the matter somewhat differently, namely in such a way that with the still unbroken natural abundance here it would be sufficient to devote about half of our time to rough work, and that the other half would remain free for beautifying work, for further education and teaching of the children. But we found so much to do that we were hardly allowed to take a few free hours."[13]

---

[12] Gottfried Duden, p. 233, quoted as in Utopia, p. 56.
[13] Friedrich Münch, Gesammelte Schriften, pp. 114 f.

That's not how they had imagined it. "We were on a tight diet. Potatoes and other vegetables, even fruit were not available at all and hardly any bread and meat were available. We grinded the not yet fully ripe, dried corn on graters we had brought with us, and from this flour the women tried to prepare various dishes with commendable inventiveness, while the hunting shotgun provided woodpeckers, squirrels, pigeons and other game. This got better after we sowed and harvested ourselves. Now there was a whole army of German children and no school. I decided to teach several days a week for a very moderate salary."[14]

In 1848, Georg Treu from Bamberg described the state of Missouri in this way in his guide for those willing to emigrate: "Missouri. Size 66,973 miles or 42,863,018 acres. Population: 383,702. The lowlands along the rivers are less healthy but fertile, producing cotton, rice, tobacco, corn and cereals in abundance; but even the higher land contains large stretches of rich soil, which is not only suitable for the cultivation of ancient cereals, but also for cattle breeding because of the rich meadows. Some farmers own two to three hundred head of cattle and four to 500 head of pigs. The country's wealth of usable metals and every kind of game is great, which means that it is not surpassed by any other part of the Union. The Missouri River and its numerous tributaries are the best place to sell the products. Trade and manufactories are already flourishing, and nowhere does the farmer lead a more pleasant and leisurely life than in this state. (...) The most excellent cities are Jefferson City with 2427

[14] Friedrich Münch, Gesammelte Schriften, pp. 114 f.

inhabitants, St. Louis with 25,810 inhabitants. The latter is already an important trading centre."[15]

Pauline Münch, who will marry Gordian Busch and have 13 children, remembers the early years in America: "When we arrived in America, my father bought a farm. But there was only a small field and a loghouse to live in. Everything else was forest. There were no close neighbors. The wilderness was still so great that you could hear the wolves howling in the evening. We children were very afraid, then. How difficult the beginning must have been for my parents who had lived completely differently in Germany. But thanks to my father's iron willpower and perseverance and the constant industriousness of my mother, who worked from morning to night, we got through the first very hard years. At that time, we lacked any convenience. All means of subsistence were expensive and we had little opportunity to get anything. Sometimes my father bought grain, but to turn it into flour you had to load a sack full on the horse and ride it a long way to the mill. There was little wheat. For us it was a feast when gridle cakes were baked. Fetching water was also difficult. It had to be carried up a long hill from a spring. How many buckets have I dragged up there in those years? But I was healthy and happy about it, because I knew it had to be that way. We had little outside help in the first few years. The first winter was particularly hard for me, as the cabin was very leaky. It didn't even have a proper foundation wall and we only had a fireplace for heating and cooking. In the evening we moved the beds to the fire, where thick

_____
[15] Treu, Ratgeber, p. 135.

wooden blocks had to burn all night. But there was a leak everywhere. When it stormed and snowed at night, there was snow on my blanket in the morning. The water that was brought in in the morning to make coffee was frozen solid. The bread had to be baked in iron pots between coals, because there was no cooking stove yet. We also had only a few pieces of furniture and the emigrant boxes had to serve as seats. We made our own shoes. (...) Now almost no one believes you anymore, but that's the way it was."[16]

Paul Follenius died of typhus in 1844, four years after his brother Karl, who died in a steamship accident near Long Island. Paul's widow Maria, who calls herself Mary in the USA, is almost destitute with her children. She writes to her sister-in-law Luise Vogt-Follen in exile in Switzerland: "How can I raise only the most necessary funds for the children's winter clothes? Julia does the hardest work in the snow and cold, but I had to leave her humble wish unfulfilled, since she has neither a coat nor anything of the kind to buy a woolen dress for Sunday. (...) My own body has been suffering steadily since last winter. I must not dwell on the thought of the situation in which we left you and Europe and what he had to get used to, and what our situation is now. Nor do I want to complain to God, if only I see and know that we can continue to exist in a decent way, as we have done so far."[17]

Continuing to exist with decency – for Friedrich Münch, this includes staying true to his ideals and going into

---

[16] Pauline Münch, private collection of Marylin H. Merrit, quoted as in Utopia, p. 157.
[17] Maria Follenius, Zentralbibliothek Zürich, Ms. Z II 420 a.3., quoted as in Rohrbach, MIId.

politics in his new homeland. Although Münch, Follenius and other men from the Giessen Emigration Society find it difficult to clear forests and work in the fields and are ridiculed as "Latin farmers", they refrain from using slaves in agriculture. "Owners of human beings" is what the clergyman calls the slave owners, and more than once he and his family are threatened with death. But like his brother Georg, he has a female slave on his farm, registered in the Federal Census of 1850, who works in the household and looks after the growing number of children. It was the only way to get a helper, his daughter Pauline states in an undated letter to her aunt in Germany when she herself is a housewife and has a slave as a maid: "It has been 2 years now since my husband bought a negro maid of 13 years (...) because you can't get any help here. I was reluctant for so long as I can't stand the thought that I would own a slave, because I have always been disgusted by this trade. Yet, what can you do, when you live in a country where such a thing is allowed, and you can't help yourself in any other way. One does such a creature a good deed, if one does as we have, buying her from a hardened sir and treating her humanely. She has it as good as our own child, she has regular meals and clothing, is handled benevolently, and of course her freedom is absent, but in its stead she has no worries."[18]

What can you do, when you live in a country where such a thing as slavery is allowed and freedom isn't for everyone? What can you do if a growing number of Americans object to immigration? Considering himself a patriot and an immigrant, devoted to equal rights and

---

[18] Pauline Münch, private collection of Marylin H. Merrit, quoted as in Utopia, p.204.

liberty, Friedrich Münch despises these self-declared "Natives" and calls them hateful and selfish. If any Americans were actually natives and not immigrants themselves, the man from Hesse points out in a speech, they would have been "the red skinned hunters, who, by the arms of the white man, have been exiled from the country of their birth." Looking back, he writes to the Germans in Missouri: "No law can take away freedom of thought from a man, and as long as one or another thing is not specifically prohibited, the freedom of speech and writing and of behaviour are guarenteed to us by the laws of the land, but in reality we were compelled to live in a state of perpetual guardianship in the hands of slave owners. Not all have felt the same way, because they were not cramped in their daily affairs and were less troubled; but no one can deny the shameful fact that in this so-called free country we were not free people, but rather had to submit to the whim of the slaveholders. Were we allowed to tell the owners of human beings what we thought of black servitude? Were we allowed to tell the slaves, or even to implicitly indicate by our conduct against them, that we regarded them as human beings and that they had human rights, too?"[19]

Thoughts are free [20]

Thoughts are free, who can guess them?
They are floating along like the shadows in the night.
No man can know them, no hunter can shoot them.
It stays as it is: Thoughts are free.

[19] Friedrich Münch, Speech July 4, p. 3. St. Charles Democrate, St. Charles, Missouri, 27. März 1862, quoted as in Utopia, p. 219.
[20] Die Gedanken sind frei (Thoughts are free, first stanza), Duo EigenArt from Nidderau and audience at the Weidig Weekend in Ober-Gleen, 2015.

Other members of the Giessen Emigration Society– such as the reform pedagogue Georg Bunsen from Frankfurt upon Main or Cornelius Schubert from Dessau – prefer to opt for a state without slavery. Cornelius Schubert for example, settles in Belleville, Illinois, and in 1847, together with his wife Louisa and others, founds a communist commune in Missouri, the "Sociality" in Atchison County. It doesn't last long, and so the Schuberts move back to Illinois. In 1862, their son Oswald is killed in the Civil War. Among thousands of other German immigrants who fought on the side of the northern states in Missouri, were also two of Friedrich Münch's sons. The younger one, Berthold, died in the battle of Springfield in 1861. "He was such a youthful boy, not even eighteen years old, of pure, noble and true mind. Still so young, he wanted to take the opportunity to join his elder brother in battle", Friedrich Münch writes in an article that is published under the title "Sacrifice for a good cause". And he points out: "Every one of the millions of souls of traitors which we have in this country is complicit in the spilled blood and the illimitable dispair."[21]

That emigrants should not transfer their view of the world to their new homeland was vehemently advocated by Georg Treu in his 1848 guidebook. The author says he had traveled the American continent for a good 20 years, and tries to convert his compatriots to the the American way of life: "The American thinks he is higher, happier, freer, more skilful than the European, and whoever interferes in this prejudice will not get away with it. Anyone who emigrates with the idea of being able to live there as a

[21] As quoted as in „Utopia", pp. 222 f.

European is (...) on the wrong path. If he even thinks that he can shine there with his education, spread enlightenment, in short, let his light shine, it will fail in most cases. (...) Furthermore, it cannot be repeated often enough that anyone who wants to go to America has to speak the language there in a finished and unbiased manner in order to get along to some extent. (...) The German language there, like the Irish, is considered a jargon of the meanest rabble."[22]

It is precisely the question of slavery that is explosive. Georg Treu states: "Already in the southern and western American states, which keep slaves, (...) the contrast between American and European idiosyncrasies is even more obvious. (...) Whoever wants or has to live there is strongly advised to acclimate in every respect (...). The slavery of the Negroes and half-breeds (...) gives the local way of life a certain immorality. (...) Whatever one may be of opinion in this respect, everyone feels that the traveler who stays for a time in slave countries or who seeks his bread there (...) does not have the right to preach his philanthropic principles on the plantations (I have seen such imprudence)."

The author from Bamberg was apparently not an ardent supporter of the German Social Revolution or sees himself as a diplomat: "What would have been said about this in the good times of feudalism in Germany if a traveller passing through or one who was looking for employment had admonished the hereditary ruler to abolish his concubines and not to abolish the subjects so inhumanely.

---

[22] Georg Treu, pp. 222 ff.

Suffice it to advise that every foreigner who enters regions where slaves are kept must submit completely to this abomination, and, as in Russia against the serfs, observe the customary procedure.[23] If you can't bring such things over your heart, stay away. In an emergency, he must often be able to look at the cruel chastisement as coldly as the planter himself, for if a white man shows pity to a black man, then the black man considers the punishment to be unjust. It is not at all difficult to sow the seed of indignation among these unfortunates. Let no one misunderstand me, because I am honestly presenting the matter as it is. I know from experience how dangerous it is to interfere in these sad conditions in countries and on islands where slaves are kept and to want to play the philanthropist; I warn every young person against such interference."[24]

Georg Treu does not want to come across as an advocate of human trafficking under any circumstances: "Slavery is an unnatural condition: all reasonable slave-owners themselves admit this, and very many wish that they could cultivate their plantations with day laborers without slaves, but as soon as they admit this, there are also a lot of harsh coercive measures and established customs, for example, the separation of social connections according to color, so that a veritable caste system arises, in a way, excused. I have never been a plantation owner; only individual Negroes I have called mine, and have never treated them differently than as one is accustomed to treat free servants. I reckon it fortunately that I have never been

---

[23] Georg Treu, p. 204. [24] Georg Treu, p. 206.

put in a position to have to keep a number of these unfortunates."

Nevertheless, he says about the blacks: "The enjoyment of freedom has little appeal for these people at all, because free negroes are precisely those who suffer the most hardship everywhere. (...) It is true that in Europe as a whole there is still a very wrong idea of the individuality of Negroes and coloured people; there is no more self-indulgent, careless, indolent people than them, and this alone reveals the utter futility of these philanthropic plans. So if you want to live and get along in those parts, you have to get used to looking at the Negroes from the point of view from which they are usually viewed in those parts—as human beasts of burden, as it were, and unfortunately you get used to it easily."[25]

Friedrich Münch does not let threats or advice stop him from taking action against slavery. In November 1864, he and his friend Arnold Krekel from Langenfeld in the Rhineland are elected delegates to the Missouri General Assembly. German radicals like them set the tone here. At the top of the agenda of the constituent meeting in St. Louis is the abolition of slavery. Arnold Krekel signs it on 11 January 1865. Shortly thereafter, as a senator, Friedrich Münch introduces a law that makes it possible for blacks to go to school. Arnold Krekel demands that they also be given the right to vote. But that is also too radical for some radicals. The vote on the Constitution in July 1865 is decided by the soldiers of the Union Army, and thus by many German-Americans.

---

[25] Georg Treu, p. 206.

The plan for a German model state in the USA, "even in a small way", did not work out. The Münch family, however, has left many traces in American history, in politics, in viticulture, in the history of the Civil War and the fight against slavery. The documentary "Utopia" by Peter Roloff, following the traces of the Giessen Emigration Society in Germany and the U.S., had its world premiere at the St. Louis International Film Festival in 2014. In Germany, it is a school film by now, a lesson in the history of democracy. More or less in reaction to it, the book "The Historic 1830s German Immigration to Missouri" has been published soon afterwards. Among the authors is the great-great-great grandson of Friedrich Münch, James F. Muench[26]. His ancestor, a dedicated follower of philosopher Immanuel Kant, and others of the Giessen Emigration Society hadn't been looking to build a utopia, he states, "but were simply searching for freedom, just like the immigrants of today". Friedrich Münch followed Kant's maxim to treat others at all times as you want to be treated yourself, which meant, for example, to fight slavery. In the dialect of Upper Hesse, Münch's homeregion in Germany, the maxim would sound like this, sung to the melody of "Go Down Moses" by Monika Felsing in the dialect of Ober- Gleen, a village close to Nieder-Ohmen in Upper Hesse, Germany, the sound of Münch's Heimat:

Woas dir käis duh soll,
doas sollsde aach kemm duh!
Gugg derr jeden eenzenn oo,
dann leannsde woas dèzu!

---

[26] Email by Jim Münch from July 22, 2023, and https://www.jamesfmuench.com.

Translation:

What no one shall do to you,
you shall not do to anyone!
Treat everyone as an individual,
and you will learn something, then.

The history of the German immigrants in Missouri is of international interest: In 2019, a graduate research seminar of the Universities of Missouri-Kansas City, Missouri-St. Louis and Hamburg led to the book "German migration to Missouri" that is online. Descendants of Friedrich Münch have joined forces to form the Münch Family Association. The longtime family's genealogist, Karl Muench, a retired professor of medicine who died in 2023, had found out that family Münch not only had sympathies for Lincoln, but is also related to the Roosevelts by marriage. Marie Münch Follenius, the sister of Friedrich and Georg Münch, had nine children, as did her daughter Mathilda Follenius Lange. Mathilda's daughter Adelheid Lange has made a name for herself as a cubist sculptor. In 1905, the 26-year-old married the filmmaker Cornelius Louis Andre Roosevelt, a cousin of Theodore Roosevelt. Leila Roosevelt, Adelheid's daughter, marries the photographer Armand Denis, with whom she makes films in Africa, among other places.

Little do we know about the women of the Giessen Emigration Society and about so many other female pioneers. Have they even been asked by their husbands or fathers if they wanted to leave their hometowns? Here is a song to the melody of "God save the King", see

"Brüder, so kann's nicht gehn", lyrics by Monika Felsing, a translation of her Upper Hessian version:

Sisters, it isn't fair!

Sisters, it isn't fair!
How we wished to stay here,
but they don't care!
We're just giving birth,
don't leave a trace on earth!
Work is what we deserve,
Here, everywhere!

Sister in your blue skirt,
sister of whom I heard,
we go abroad!
Soon we will be at sea,
for an eternity
no one will think of thee!
His story told!
Sisters, our brothers still
always do have their will
and we do not!
We dream of speaking out,
also want to be proud,
and so let's say it loud:
Freedom's our lot!

The Missouri Germans Consortium and others uphold the memory of the early immigrants. The professional genealogist and award-winning author Dorris Keeven-Franke for example has been location manager for the documentary film "Utopia", co-author of the book "Utopia. Revisiting a German State in America" and part of the international cultural project "Travelling Summer Republic". Her passion is sharing local history, also women's history, as she does in her program "Pauline's Diary". Pauline Busch née Münch, the daughter of Friedrich Münch and his first wife, who suffered several strokes of fate, has left behind letters and a journal. Her story "is similar to thousands of German women who emigrated here in the 19th Century", Dorris Keeven-Franke says.

And what had it been like for Louise Münch, who had just lost her father and two of her brothers and had almost died in postpartum after the birth of her first child, to go on such an arduous journey with a baby? How might it have been for her to start anew in the wilderness, to lose four of their twelve children in infancy, their 18-year-old son Berthold in the civil war, to build a farm and provide for a growing family? It needs great imagination to guess how it felt. Well, her husband tried – in his guidebook "Der Staat Missouri" ("The State of Missouri, described with particular regard to German immigration") that he published for German immigrants in 1859 and presented it on a promotional tour through Germany and Switzerland. It was "a book to prepare prospective German emigrants so they might better adjust to the New World after they arrived", the late historian Siegmar Muehl wrote in the Yearbook of German American Studies of 1998. And Münch's advice was offered mainly to male concerns. "One exception occurred in the chapter on country life", Siegmar Muehl stated. "Here, he set forth the prospects

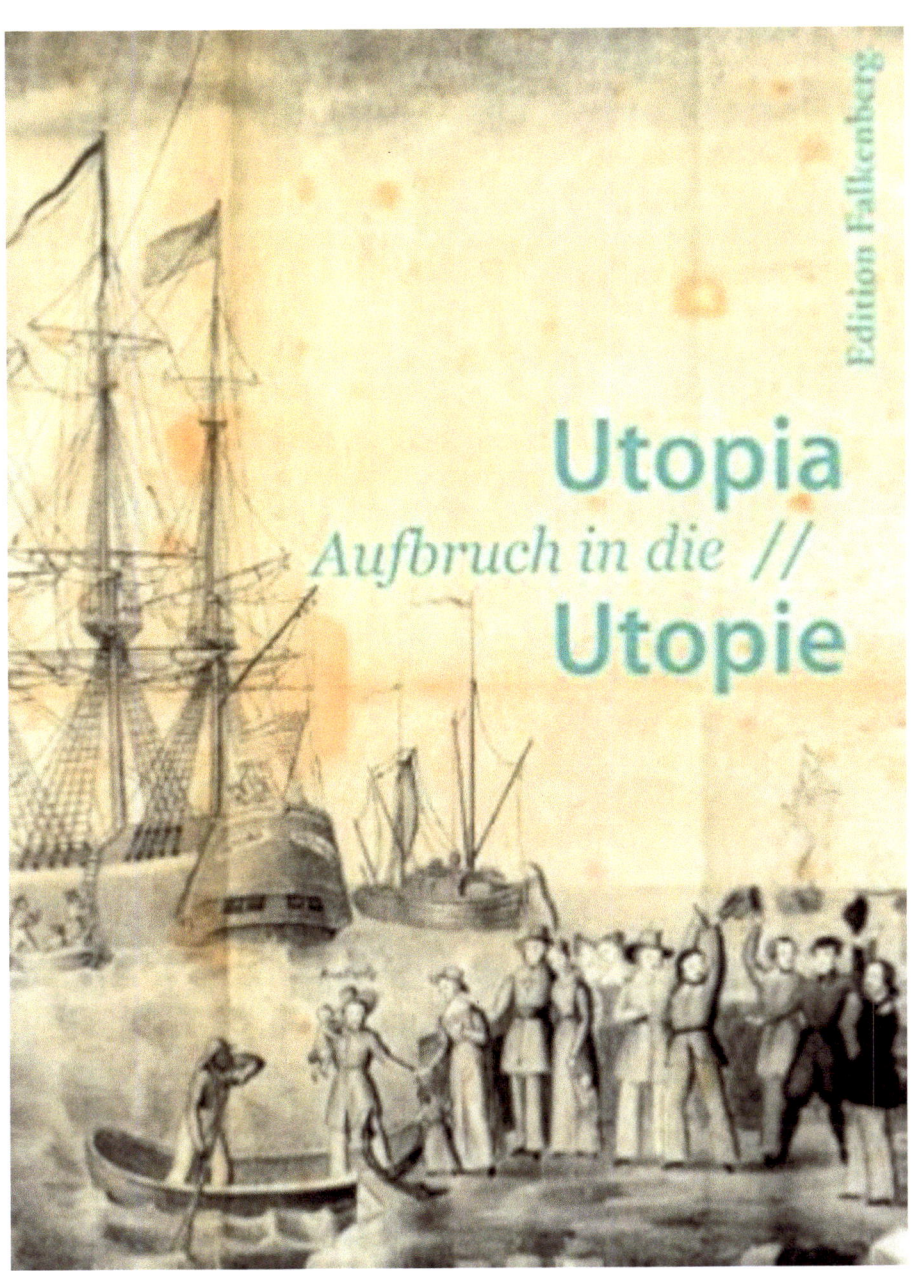

Edition Falkenberg

Utopia

Aufbruch in die //

Utopie

The book about the Giessen Emigration Society.

of the immigrant wife as someone sharing in the experiences of farm living."[27]

"A man can be satisfied only if his wife is as well", Friedrich Münch wrote. "Many wives, if they have to live in the country, are made uncomfortable, partly by what they left behind, partly by what is demanded of them. Yet the great majority of German wives adjust with a good and ready will to the new situation. Our wives have significant and difficult tasks here. In performing these, they feel important, are never plagued by boredom and are satisfied by what they accomplish for their family. They keep their house clean and orderly, do the cooking, baking, washing, knitting, mending, sewing (some make men's clothing better than a tailor), care for children, milk the cows, make butter, cheese and soap, dry the fruit, cook jams, prepare fruit and vegetables, tend the flower and kitchen gardens and the fowl. Indeed, many even weave the necessary fabrics for household use. (...) Despite all that, wives do not cease to live as cultured human beings. They are the center of the intimate and warm family life."[28]

From 1866, Münch's guidebook is published in Bremen, first by Müller, and the second edition by Hauschild in 1875. Two decades have passed since the book came out. Farm life has become a bit easier, also for women. Though they are still not plagued by boredom. The mentioned machines don't run by electricity, yet. And every helping hand is needed.

---

[27] Friedrich Münch, Gesammelte Schriften, pp. 113 and 122.
[28] Münch, Der Staat Missouri, 1859, S. 38, quoted as in Muehl. Münch, Gesammelte Schriften, pp. 113 and 122.

"The German housewives usually enjoy very functional ovens, which have a device for frying, baking bread and cakes and heating larger amounts of water", Friedrich Münch wrote. "They are satisfied with the local cookware, washing machines, milking equipment, preserving cans, among other things, and ensure that there is always a lot on the table. (...) Good cellars are a real amenity, and even more and more ice houses and bath houses are being built. Despite some relief, the tasks of the local farmer's wife are not small. Rough work in the field and the barn is not to be expected of her; but she keeps her house clean and her garden in order, takes care of cooking, washing, sewing (recently with the help of the sewing machine), spinning (wool only), knitting, fruit drying, the poultry and the dairy industry, cooks her soap, feeds the children and yet is ready in time as, from early on, all the family members help to the best of their ability to cope. Thus she does not become dull or peasant, but rather finds the necessary free hours for social recreation. The girls have grown up in the fifteenth year, and then we rarely keep them longer than a couple of years."[29]

In the emigrant novel "Jürnjakob Swehn der Amerikafahrer", at least the first-person narrator, a pioneer, does not feel superior to the women in his family. The emigrant Carl Wiedow from Mecklenburg who had come to Victor, Iowa, with his wife in 1868, kept writing letters to his former teacher. The teacher's son, Johannes Gillhoff, made a successful novel out of it in 1917, which was soon read also in Hessian villages. In more than one chapter the quick-witted wife called Wieschen and the equally quick-

[29] Münch, Der Staat Missouri, 1875, pp. 98. f.,

witted daughter have the last word: "Well, now I am smoking my pipe, and my wife, Wieschen scolds me: The smoke makes their stores look yellowish. Wieschen, I say, how could the black smoke of my brown pipe make your white curtains yellow? And she says: Jürnjakob, how is it possible that the black cow of our farmer eats green grass and gives white milk and yellow butter? And my daughter says: How is it possible, dad, that the brightest flashes come from the darkest clouds? So, I had my answers. Don't mess with that women people! Really, they are a completely different nation, the ones that have long hair."[30]

A completely different nation... Friedrich Münch of the Giessen Emigration Society sees things a little differently. In 1848, the year of the St. Paul's Church Assembly in Frankfurt am Main, he writes an essay in Missouri on the social position and rights of women. Die Muench Family Association has documented the speech:[31] "They tell us a great deal about "Emancipation of Woman," as though she was held by man in an unworthy state of dependence, while in a thousand instances our compassion should rather be on the side of Man, who seems to need being emancipated not less than his fair and all-powerful complement. But of a full equality of the natural desti-nation of Man and Woman, an equality of their position

[30] Gillhoff, Jürnjakob Swehn, der Amerikafahrer. More about Carl Wiedow (1847-1913) and his wife Elisabeth, including a photo of the family: https://de.findagrave.com/memorial/146962830/carl-wiedow.

[31] Friedrich Münch, Aufsatz über die gesellschaftliche Stellung und die Rechte von Frauen, Missouri 1848. The Muench Family Association has put the text online on https://www.muenchfamilyassociation.com/german-immigrant-women.html. Also for the following quotations.

in life, an equality of their rights and duties, very few, I guess, have as yet dreamed. Nature has not willed such a thing. The destination of every creature is shown forth by the native properties it was endowed with by its Maker; the rights of every human individual are corresponding with certain duties. Now I do not say, that Woman's destination, position in life, rights, and duties are inferior to those of Man, but different, greatly different. This difference extends even to the moral sphere. Tolerance, for instance, although a praiseworthy virtue, can, if carried too far, become blamable feebleness in Man under circumstances, when Woman might be still justified, nay, morally obliged to exercise it. In short, the scene of action for either sex is distinctly marked by nature. Woman's greatest perfections can only be manifested in Domestic life, Man's in public – Man, of course, rules by the power of physical strength, prowess, and intelligence; Woman reigns by the irresistibility of love, innocence, tact, fineness, delicacy, in short, amiability. And who can say, which of both kinds of dominion is stronger or nobler?"

Here the Protestant pastor, ahead of his time in so many ways, but also a child of his time, speaks of the God-ordained order. "Man is not superior to Woman, nor is she to Man. The truth is, neither of them represents the entire fulness of human perfection, but they are designed to do so by and in their union. They are not equal, but congenial. I must confess, that in the course of my life I never met a woman, virgin or wife, who seriously wished this natural order of things subverted. The more refined woman is, the more she thinks of the high calling of her own sex, of its duties. I therefore say: A Woman should not have a direct voice or hand in the enactment and administration of our laws. She is represented by her father, husband et cetera. He is a mean lawgiver, who, in the enactment of laws does not consult the natural rights, honor, and welfare of both sexes equally."

So no right to vote for women? "I candidly believe that the female half of our population is better represented now in this very republic, than if females should make their appearance on the floor of Congress and General Assemblies, or take the Presidential chair, et cetera", Friedrich Münch wrote. "Let us be *men*, real men, and we shall find means to cure all present evils and wants of our public affairs. In fact, this very state we live in, is undoubtedly better governed than any other in the world. I know that we still labor under many imperfections. I say with all the firmness of religious conviction, if you truly value the lovely and charming properties of female character, keep your wives and daughters far from those scenes of life which might tend in the least to violate the delicacy of their feelings, the purity of their hearts."

That's how most men in their old homeland keep it. In 1848, Hessian women are no real citizens, they have no right to vote in the National Assembly of St. Paul's Church, the first all-German parliament. Women are not allowed to participate in the discussion, nor are they allowed to stand for election. What remains for them is to follow the men's debates from the "ladies' gallery" and interject. They are denied the lectern, the place in a parliament even until after the First World War. In the 21st century, the American Ruth Stern Gasten, a victim of Nazi persecution and an emigrant from Nieder-Ohmen, has mentioned a

Portrait of Friedrich Ludwig Weidig in the museum in Kirtorf.

motto of her life in the epilogue of her biography "An Accidental American": "Democracy is not a spectator sport."

Die Gedanken sind frei (Thoughts are free). Duo Eigen Art and audience at the Weidig Weekend in Ober-Gleen, 2015. Full version in German.

Zweiback and Captain's Dinner

How a five-year-old and a seventeen-year-old from Hesse experienced their first sea voyage and what became of them and others

Disappeared the beach,
disappeared the land,
ship on the high seas.
All around us are waves and sea,
that is all I see.
Swaying the waves,
seagulls flying homewards.
Golden shines the sun, hearts full of bliss,
homeland, goodbye! [1]

Let's accompany two young people from Hesse on their first sea voyage: We will meet Edmund, a Melsunger who worked his way up from ship's boy to captain and later escaped the largest civilian nautical disaster in German waters. First we will meet Ruth, a seaworthy five-year-old from Nieder-Ohmen, who experienced her family's escape from Nazi Germany in 1939 as an adventure.

Ruth Stern Gasten[2]: "Hamburg! Hamburg! This is the final stop of this train! Everybody off!" the conductor shouted.

---

[1] "Heute an Bord" (On board today), a sailor's song from the 19th Century, the composer is unknown, the German lyrics were written by Paul Vollrath in 1903

[2] This and the following parts of Ruth's story are from Ruth Stern Gasten, „An Accidental American".

Along with hundreds of other passengers in their muted winter coats, hats and scarves, my father in his bulky brown overcoat and my mother in her dark blue one disembarked into the train station. Papa was carrying two large suitcases and Mama two smaller ones. Papa set his down on the platform, turned to the train and lifted me off the top step. I, too, was wearing a warm coat to ward off the January chill. Mine was maroon and flared out at the waist. Mama had bought it in Giessen, and I thought it was ever so pretty. I was sleepy and disoriented. My mother had packed lots of food for the nine-hour trip from Nieder-Ohmen to Hamburg, the seaport where we were to board the ship that would sail to America. Some dark bread, yellow cheese, and a shiny red apple helped me to regain some of my five-year-old interest in everything that was happening around me."

So they sold their belongings, said goodbye to friends and relatives, and then left their small village in the Vogelsberg with a heavy heart. Like many Jewish men, Josef Stern had been in a concentration camp after the pogrom night of 1938. With the little that he, his wife Hanna and his daughter Ruth are allowed to take with them, they reach Hamburg. As Jewish emigrants, they have to endure final checks, harassment and humiliation before they can leave Germany and are finally out of danger.

Ruth Stern Gasten: "Along with other suitcase-laden passengers, we were herded on to buses that were bound for the ship dock. All of us were Germans who were fleeing because of Hitler's persecutions. There were people who openly disagreed with the regime – professors, writers,

Ruth Stern as a child in Nieder-Ohmen, Upper Hesse.

homosexuals, and, of course, Jews. The bus stopped at an enormous square building that must have been a warehouse once. The building had been turned into a center for examining the luggage and bodies of the departing refugees to make sure they didn't take anything valuable out of the country. I remember the experience as being humiliating. I can only imagine how it was for my parents. My mother and I were directed to an area for women. There the uniformed officials were women. After we went through the gauntlet and had put on our clothes again, we were told to exit by the door in front of us. I looked straight ahead and saw a huge ship. It looked like it was big enough to hold all the people from Nieder-Ohmen, and from Giessen, too. Papa told me that it was called the 'S. S. Deutschland'. I could hardly wait to get on this floating city."

Edmund Valentin Badenhausen, one of the eight children of Philipp and Eleonore Badenhausen, nee Schiricke is 17 years old and far from being of legal age when he leaves Melsungen in 1857. And he goes alone. The young man from North Hesse joins the Hamburg-Amerikanische Packetfahrt-Actien-Gesellschaft, or Hapag, also called the Hamburg-America Line. He writes letters in diary form and sends them to his parents, asking them to carefully preserve the letters so that they can be published later. His granddaughter Ida Hase has translated the one remaining letter. On October 11, 1857, the 17-year-old wrote: "On October 2nd, the anxiously awaited packet ship 'Oder' arrived here, after a very fast trip from New York, taking only 27 days. I immediately introduced myself to the inspector of American Packet Ship Association and

Ruth Stern Gasten with her book and the translated version in 2017.

there I met, by good fortune and chance, my present Captain. This man appealed to me immediately, for he was very kind; in fact, his manner showed a strong character. I was told to come back, which I did, and there again found my Captain, just as though he had been waiting for me. The inspector wrote down on a slip of paper the equipment which I needed. The Captain took the paper and went with me, the future ship's boy – think of my surprise –, the top man and the most menial of all, to the store keeper, who filled my needs, and asked when I wanted to come on board. When I told him I wanted to come on board right away, he was satisfied."[3]

Edmund returns to family Bessen who had taken care of him in Hamburg, so kindly that he can hardly find words to express it. The other day, his cousin Wilhelm acompanied him to the ship. But the pilot just looks Edmund all over with a sarcastic smile. He hasn't learned yet how to work, he tells him, and that he would accept him as a ship's boy only if he had a certificate from the inspector. As soon as Edmund has the certificate, he is then accepted. He goes on board and stands there like an abandoned one. The pilot, the sailors and the ship's boys ignore the new one completely, no one shows him where his place on board will be, or where he should change his clothes in order to go to work or where he should sleep.

"When I asked, no one listened and the sailors made fun of me", Edmund wrote to his beloved ones. "A

---

[3] This and the next parts of his Edmund's story are from the letter that Ida Asterita Hase had translated.

Captain Edmund Badenhausen from Melsungen.
The photo was taken by C. Fr. Schönborn in Ruhla/Thuringia.

Hundredweight was on my heart and I almost cried out loud. Then finally a sympathetic soul took pity on me, namely the cook's helper who aided me to take my things into the cabin where the sailors have their place, where they eat, sleep and do everything. There I quickly dressed and asked the head pilot what I should do. He sent me to polish. I had to polish the compass, all the tin-work which re-enforced the ship, and the two bells. That lasted until four o'clock. Then I helped with the loading. Then I helped get the cargo out of the way. That lasted until 5:30 p.m. Then it was time to eat. The food was potatoes stewed with onions, tea or milk and sugar, pumpernickel and Zweiback. Rye bread tastes like matzo and must lie in the tea a long time until it gets soft. Also butter, that is butter that stinks, which the others spread on their bread thickly, but I just scratched it on the bread."

Ruthchen Stern also enters a new world. The crew treats all passengers equally, there is no sign of the anti-Semitism they experienced in Germany. And for a small, inquisitive girl, there is so much to discover: "Picture this scenario. You are a five-year-old child, born and raised in a tiny provicial German town in the 1930's, and you find yourself on an ocean liner – the world's largest playground. Think about it. An ocean liner has finite boundaries; so you can't really get lost. The dangerous areas on the ship have locked doors or big red "Do Not Enter" signs to keep out passengers. So much to look at and learn about: the wide, richly carpeted staircases that led from one deck to another and then to the staterooms; the game rooms where adults played chess, cards, and other games; the inviting children's play room with its wind-up toys, games, large pillows, dolls and animals of all sizes and shapes; the salons with large windows overlooking the top deck where the grownups had cocktails, snacks, and talked to each other. Best of all was the beautiful dining room with its lovely crystal chandeliers. The tablecloths on the round tables were white linen damask. The water goblet at each place setting had a pastel color napkin arranged in it. In the center of each table was a small cut glass bowl of fresh flowers. What an amazing variety of places for a child to explore!"

There had never been so much luxury in Upper Hesse.

Ruth Stern Gasten: "On the ship's deck, I noticed smiling young men in dark blue uniforms and crisp white shirts scattered about. Each of them had a long sheet of paper in his hand. One of them strode up to us and said: "Welcome aboard the "Deutschland". I'm Erich. Tell me your name, and I'll show you to your cabin." He took Mama's two suitcases with a swift friendly gesture, and led us towards the middle of the ship. And then Erich said "Here we are. Cabin 396, your quarters for the next week. I will be your steward. If you need anything, let me know; and I'll do my best to get it." He opened the door to the stateroom, a compact room where everything was neat and orderly. There were two regular size beds and a small one for me underneath the little round window that Erich called a porthole. Even a closet, two night tables and a small bath. I was fascinated when I noticed that everything was attached to the walls or to the floor. I soon found out why."

Back to Hamburg, 1857. When the work on board is done, the sailors go ashore to spend their wages after the long crossing. The new cabin boy stays behind. Where should he sleep? Someone shows him a berth, which he has to share with another boy. The other one is sick, his bloody, sweaty mattress has been thrown overboard. Since then, he has been sleeping on naked boards. "He looks awfully dirty and ugly. He seldomly washes himself. And this is now my sleeping companion", Edmund Badenhausen wrote in his letter. "Now I have fixed up my bed. A hard mattress of seaweed and a light horse blanket, that's my bed. At 8 o'clock, all lights must be out on all ships in the Hamburg harbor. Then everyone squeezes and crowds himself into bed. I fell asleep, and even in my sleep I still heard the lapping of the waves against the bow of the boat, for the sailor's quarters are in the front of the ship."

For Edmund Badenhausen, the first night on board begins. It ends at six o'clock. He writes to his parents and everyone else who will read it: "The next morning I awoke feeling as though I had taken a beating. That can be easily imagined for one goes to bed dressed, namely with a blue woolen undershirt, a blue and white striped undershirt, white woolen underpants and woolen stockings which reach above the knee. During the day, there is added to that heavy sailor's shoes and a sailer's knife on a plaid belt, drawn about the body. To that also a Scot's cap, very much like the bishop's hat, and pants of gray leather. That is my costume."

In 1857, the ship's boy learns that it is not customary to say "good morning" on board, either with the pilot or the

Dimmers

1018 WASHINGTON ST.
HOBOKEN, N.J.
FORMERLY IN NEW YORK.

Catharina (Schoemer) Badenhausen, Edmund's wife.
The photo was taken in Hoboken by Dimmers.

Captain. He washes himself in a bucket of water and gets his first breakfast. "We drank coffee without milk or anything. After, there was bacon, pumpernickel and Zweiback", he notes. "Then the work began. I cleaned and polished in the morning. Breakfast was served at 8 o'clock, the same as we ate at 6 o'clock. Inspite of the work, I was extremely bored and terribly homesick. The happy days gone by passed in my mind. I thought of you, dear parents, the unforgettable hours of parting, the solitious advice, receiving father's blessing, the loving lingering and nodding up to the window as I went over the market square. I could barely keep back my tears. All watch me while I work, and even now, while I write this, my tears are plentiful thinking of my dear parents, relatives and friends. Away from home, one realizes rightly why parents, brothers, sisters and home are so dear and beloved, what a treasure one has left behind when one is among total strangers who don't have a single word of sympathy. They even ridicule the tears of one who thinks of his dear loved ones, and order one to work, with mockery and curses. This is especially true for the sailors. They cause each other grief and a seaman must beware of them, he must have a strong character."

We hover

*Yes, we hover, yes, we hover
over the great blue sea.
Yes, we hover, and have just been
in the shallow water here.*

*Great blue plains, great blue plains
expand wide before our eyes.*

Great blue plains, great blue plains,
between us and paradise.

Yes, we hover, yes, we hover,
Horses drag us overseas,
Horses that do live in heaven,
they're called wind and don't eat hay.

Yes, we hover, yes, we hover,
our way's invisible.
But we hover, yes, we hover,
On this big ship overseas.

We are dreaming, we are dreaming
of lands on the horizon,
where we'll all be foreigners, first,
home of tribes that aren't our own.

Yes, we hover, yes, we hover,
like gods, over the dike.
In a land that's rich in dreams,
we long for a better live.[*]

The "Deutschland", on which the Stern family travels to New York in 1939, gets into heavy seas, as Ruth Stern Gasten recalls in her book: "The ship had just started its voyage to Southampton, England. The wind had picked up. The waves were high, and the ship was rolling. After I had been on the top deck, when I opened the door of

---

[*] Lyrics written by Monika Felsing to the rhythm of "I am sailing" by Rod Stewart, about migration, about the feeling of being on board of a ship and sliding into the great blue. The cover song is originally in Upper Hessian dialect, under the title "Joa, mir schwewe".

the cabin, I noticed my mother was lying on the bed, and her face was pale. Papa greeted me and explained, "Your Mama seems to be a little seasick. She'll probably feel better after she eats." That was not to be. Mama didn't get better. She got worse and worse. I, on the other hand, was well and happy. The North Atlantic storms left me completely unaffected. The wind howled, and icy hail pummeled the deck and made noise as it hit the portholes. I enjoyed it all. The decks rolled when you walked on them. Just another challenge for a five-year-old. By midweek, Papa was affected, too. Erich came to the rescue. He told the Captain about my plight; and that very evening, I ate at the Captain's table. What fun it was! The young officers and other guests questioned me and even listened to my responses. I told them about my Uncle Meier and my Aunt Hedwig and my two cousins. I told them how much I loved Rosie, the cow. I told them how the government had taken away my developmentally slow aunt and put her in a hospital and how I hoped she had made friends there. I felt ever so important and grownup, in fact, the most important I ever felt in my first five years of life. And I'll tell you something that Mama never found out. The Captain and his friends would let me eat two or even three desserts if I wanted them. Mama NEVER let me do that. I kind of felt sorry for my parents, but I had such a good time eating at the captain's table, and being able to go where I wanted that I secretly wished them to stay sick."

Many people struggle with seasickness on their first voyage, but even experienced sailors can be affected by it. The problem is: The eyes transmit to the brain that the

94

body is at rest, and through the vestibular organ in the inner ear, muscles and joints perceive movement. Who is right? There is dizziness and nausea, blurred vision and headaches, sweating and other symptoms, up to circulatory collapse and death wish. Seasick people vomit because their body interprets this as poisoning based on the symptoms and wants to get rid of the stomach contents as quickly as possible. In the 21st century, medical professionals recommend "antihistamines, which should be taken at least four hours before taking off, and parasympatholytics, but also vitamin C, ginger, acupressure tapes, fresh air, concentrated work, warm clothing. It is important to look to the horizon, stay in the middle of the ship, drink enough water, sleep and eat light meals, for example fruits and vegetables, raw carrots, soups, Zweiback, chamomile, peppermint and ginger tea. On the list of foods that seasick people should better avoid are histamine-containing foods such as salami, hard cheese, sauerkraut, tomatoes, strawberries, spinach, chocolate, snacks, walnuts, bananas, coffee, black tea, green tea and alcohol".

Up to 90 percent of people are said to be susceptible to seasickness, including people who have been at sea for a long time. Only children under the age of two never get seasick, says the volunteer sea rescue doctor Dr. Jens Kofahl from the Deutsche Gesellschaft zur Rettung Schiffbrüchiger (DGzRS, German Society for the Rescue of Shipwrecked Persons) in Cuxhaven, who is quoted on the DGzRS website[5]. In his 1897 guide to Canada, Heinrich

[5] The physician Dr. Jens Kofahl, Deutsche Gesellschaft zur Rettung Schiffbrüchiger (DGzRS, German Society for the Rescue of Shipwrecked Persons), Cuxhaven, as quoted on the website of the DGzRS.

Lemcke assumed that 15- to 65-year-olds were particularly affected, rarely children or the elderly, women more often than men. "If ever suffering has been the object of human complaints, it is above all seasickness", he stated. "It is a disease in which, as they say, one cannot live or die, and it occurs in the passengers when the ship is subjected to greater fluctuations by the movements of the sea. For some, seasickness stops after a few days after the person gets used to the fluctuations of the ship. Others do not leave it during the whole journey and it only disappears again when entering the solid land."[6]

From American studies, Lemcke knows what can be done about it: Three days before the departure of their ship, travelers are supposed to take a brominated medicine after consulting a doctor. Did the author also hear that bromine was originally extracted from seaweed? He recommends a mixture of bromindes to be taken, a teaspoonful before eating and before going to bed, for three days before going on board. Ruth Stern's parents apparently do not know the remedy. And, apparently, no other. But at some point, the time of nausea comes to an end for them too.

Ruth Stern Gasten: "The night before our arrival in New York, the seas turned calm, and we awoke to much excitement on board. You could hear the passengers' footsteps in the hallways as they hurried to the top deck. No one wanted to miss seeing the Statue of Liberty. The three of us joined the climbing throng of bodies. "Look!

---

[6] Lemcke, Canada, das Land und seine Leute.

It's over there!", Papa shouted as he lifted me high. All I could see was a dark tall object far away in the water. As we watched, the Statue became the majestic figure of a woman in flowing robes holding aloft a flaming torch and welcoming us to the United States, as she had welcomed so many immigrants before us. As we walked down the slanting gangway, I thought of the kind Captain and the friendly stewards. I felt pampered and petted, filled with delicious food, and the strong knowledge that there are lots of good people in the world. What a glorious adventure! I was ready to start life in America."

And what does the young Melsunger learn on his first crossing? The life of a sailor is hard: "Tell Brill that he should stay in the fatherland and earn an honest living there. I can assure him that work on the outside is much harder, as he can see from my letter. Should I ever be lucky enough to sail as Captain and shall have saved something, then I shall return to Hesse to await my last days there. There is no place more beautiful than where one's home is. If I should happily come home to Melsungen after my second trip, you will find me completely changed. The sea air is doing me no end of good."

The ship's boy actually becomes a Captain: Edmund Badenhausen attends the seamen's school in Hamburg, gets his officer's commission and becomes first officer, then Captain of the mail steamer "Frisia". From 1878 he captains the steamer "Cimbria" of Hapag, which is used on the passage from Hamburg to New York. After Badenhausen rescues the crew of the schooner "Julia and

Mary" from distress at sea, U.S. President Rutherford B. Hayes sends him a gold watch. Tsar Alexander II awards the Hessian captain with a medal for rescuing Russian sailors from a sinking ship. At the age of 41, Edmund Badenhausen emigrates to the United States as the Hapag and the Lloyd have offered him another responsible position at their piers in New York. In February 1883, he becomes Superintendent of the new pier of Hapag in Hoboken in New York Harbor. The Captain from Hesse will never see his hometown Melsungen again. He settles in New Jersey with his wife Catharina Marie, née Schoemer, who is called Tini B, his two daughters and three sons. His granddaughter Ida Hase told her cousin Bayard Badenhausen about the crossing, as remembered by her mother Carola. The letter, written in 1959, can be read in the blog Badmorgen by Susan Eldridge, Bayard's daughter.[7]

Ida Hase: "Mother often told me about the stormy trip, how the stewards were sloshing about the dining room in their boots; how the deck chairs slid back and forth against the railing, etc. Uncle Henry was a tiny baby at the time and Mother said he was bedded in a little box."[8]

While Edmund Badenhausen was Hapag's Inspector of the Harbor in Hoboken, Gustav Freiherr von Berg from Hungary also went ashore there with his daughter and a governess. His letters from 1893 were published the year

---

[7] Blog Badmorgen of Susan Eldridge nee Badenhausen, and the article of Herbert Simon about emigrants from Melsungen.

[8] Memories of Ida Hase on Badmorgen, as well as the later quotations.

after his return under the title "To my loved ones in the homeland". In the preface he writes: "At the age of 65, traveling is never pleasant, especially if you have an eighteen-year-old daughter who has a pronounced talent and special penchant for long journeys. If her wish had been the only decisive factor, we would now be sitting in Alaska, Japan or the East Indies. Old memories are awakened in me, at the age of eighteen I traveled for the first time on a railway from Harzburg to Braunschweig on the feast of Pentecost. Today, every four-year-old child has already traveled several thousand kilometers. Enfin, you have to take the new zeitgeist into account: Mimi accompanies me. But alone? It's going to be harder! Miss Pattison from London, who had been in our house for a long time, offered to go along.""

Of course, they do not travel in the tween deck of the "Spree". On board is a famous American veil dancer, Miss Fuller from Fullersburg in Illinois, who performs for the benefit of the sailors' fund. After nine days of sailing, the "Spree" is approaching New York, Hoboken and Bedloes Island, which will be later known as Ellis Island.

"The first piece of earth we saw was Sandy Hook Bar with a lighthouse. We sailed through the white and red Gedney Channel, then through the Narrows, and the most magnificent harbor picture in the world lay before our surprised eyes", Gustav, Freiherr von Berg, wrote. "In the middle, opposite us, New York, an elongated sea of houses, surrounded by a wreath of harbor squares, piers that strongly remind of the primeval forests of the hinterland,

---

° Gustav, Freiherr von Berg, Meine Lieben, p. 2.

everything is made of wood, still provisional, not like the ashlar-clad banks of the Danube in Budapest; huge inscriptions denote the countless steamer routes, railway lines and other things. On the right is Brooklyn, a suburb of 800,000 people, and the connecting link between the two is the Brooklyn Bridge, the largest suspension bridge in the world, almost 2000 meters long, a miracle of human acumen. On the left of Bedloes Island, we are greeted by the Statue of Liberty by August Bartholdi, the largest statue in the world; France donated it to the United States in 1886. And if we look back, a lovely picture of Long Island, New Jersey, with its wooded heights, small towns, villages, magnificent and friendly villas lies behind us, in front of us a large water mirror with ships of all countries, the largest passenger steamers, three-masts, cargo steamers, yachts, brigs, ferries with whole railroad trains or omnibuses. Ferries for passengers and wagons, the size of a city apartment building for 1000 people and 20 trucks with engines whose beamers reach above the deck and give them a peculiar expression. And then there is the ringing of the ships, their foghorns, a heathen noise. We stream past in amazement, all the way to the Hudson, which separates New York from Hoboken with 43,000 inhabitants, where our steamer lands, we are in America! With the punctuality of an express train, our "Spree" lands at 8 o'clock in the morning at the pier of the Bremen Lloyd Hoboken on the left bank of the Hudson."[10]

In Hoboken, Captain Badenhausen is very well respected. And he is known for his kindness. When he dies in New Jersey in 1902 at the age of 62, he is mourned by many

[10] Gustav, Freiherr von Berg, Meine Lieben, p. 14.

The "Cimbria", on a postcard that is part of the Badenhausen collection.

The house in the middle is the former home of
family Badenhausen in Melsungen.

people. His wife Tini B travels several times to Germany and in 1912 also visits relatives in Hesse. In 1922, she takes her 19-year-old granddaughter Ida to Europe. Ida has just graduated from high school.

"The German Mark was dropping in value constantly", Ida Hase remembered. "When we left U.S. the exchange rate was 350 marks for a dollar. By the time the ship made it to Germany it was 500 on the dollar. We had worn money-belts with gold pieces because gold was the standard. However, they did not want the gold pieces, so we exchanged regular money for the Deutsche Marks."

In 1980, a year before her death, in a letter to her great nephew Stephen, Ida wrote that she and her grandmother had put packages of notes into their wardrobe trunks and when they had dinner in a restaurant, Ida put a package under the table and put her foot on it. In the long run, it was too difficult to exchange the coins, so they had the gold pieces melted down in the W. C. Heraeus platinum smelter in Hanau. Another of Edmund's descendants, a great-granddaughter, was in Melsungen in 1984. Her first name is maritime history: Cimbria.

Cimbria

Two brothers wanted to travel
to America.
They went with many others
on the Cimbria.
The night was bright,
then the fog rose.

The ship pursued slowly
the prescribed run.
Suddenly, they saw a flash
of green light.
Help, heavens, we're sinking!
The Cimbria, it breaks.
Farewell, my brother,
I can already feel the water!
We have to drown, everyone of us.
We are all lost!
And if you don't drown
and be saved here,
then return home
and greet our people from me!
But the brother doesn't answer,
his mouth has already fallen silent,
and the waters dragged
the other one down.
Down to the ground.[11]

The Moritat from the Folk Song Archive describes the last minutes in the lives of the brothers Wilhelm and Alexander Beuth from Espa in the Taunus, who drowned in the sinking of the Cimbria. In England, the Netherlands, Northern Europe, Russia and other countries, Hessians had peddled it. The Beuth brothers drown. The wife of the pastor of Espa, Lydia Schmittborn, writes the lyrics, and young people sing them to the tune of "If you want to love, you have to suffer".

---

[11]   Lyrics by Lydia Schmittborn, Espa, 1883, as quoted in the Volksliederarchiv, and translated into English by Monika Felsing.

The accident occurs in 1883, not long after Captain Edmund Badenhausen has relinquished command of the "Cimbria". In the fog near the island of Borkum, the "Cimbria" is rammed by the English coal steamer "Sultan" and sinks within a quarter of an hour. There are 91 crew members and 401 passengers on board. Most of them are emigrants from Eastern Europe or Germans like the Beuth brothers, the 20-year-old Edmund Adolph Olbers from Cuxhaven or the 35-year-old milliner Helene Weege from Berlin, who has left her husband, and travels with her children Bertha and Alfred. Moritz Strauss, a Darmstadt toy dealer on a business trip, is also on the passenger list. The siblings Katinka, Auguste and Georg Rommer from Biberach, who want to make their fortune overseas as "Swabian songbirds". The native American "Red Jacket", his wife Sunshine, the medicine man Crowfoot and three others who want to return to the United States from a European tour[12]. Their fate inspired an unknown author and newspaper reader to write a poem that begins like this:

Sinking of the Cimbria

Shudder penetrates through all limbs,
when you read about "Cimbria".

---

[12] More about the „Cimbria": Wrack- und Fischereimuseum „Windstärke 10", Cuxhaven. The archive of the Chamber of Commerce (Handelskammer) and the Gesellschaft für Familiengeschichte e.V. (Society for Family History), MAUS, have put the passenger list of the „Johanne" online: http://www.passagierlisten.de. Since the "Verordnung wegen der Auswanderer mit hiesigen oder fremden Schiffen" of 1832, the first state law in Germany for the protection of emigrants, those lists were obligatory. Later, the Chamber of Commerce founded the "Nachweisungsbureau für Auswanderer" where Captains had to deliver their lists. From 1875 to 1907 it was allowed to destroy lists that were older than three years. Today, the archive of the Handelskammer Bremen contains 3017 of formerly more than 4500 passenger lists from 1920 to 1939. See also below.

This watch was presented to Captain Badenhausen by the President of the United States.

This steamship wanted to go back
to America.
When Cuxhaven is over,
a heavy fog descended
on the big, wide sea.
It was dark night all around. (...)

But it cannot be changed any more.
What has happened, has happened.
Deeply saddened in all countries
the people read in the paper now
what disaster has happened.
Hundreds of lives
had to end at sea.

Good Lord! The suffering is heavy,
Caution is certainly needed
on the ships as known,
the swim belt and the lifeboats
were all in good shape.
But if fate willing,
that was to go down like this
this ship with man and mouse,
Our tears burst out.[13]

Only 56 people were rescued. Almost all the women and children are among the dead. To this day, the sinking of the "Cimbria" is the greatest disaster of civil seafaring in German waters. In 1974, the wreck was found at a depth of 25 meters, 19 nautical miles northwest of the isle of Borkum. From 2001 onwards, wreck divers took out of

---

[13] Lyrics from 1883, author unknown.

the wreck what wasn't attached. In the Cuxhaven museum "Wind Force 10" the story of the "Cimbria" is told, in the Melsungen archive and in the blog Badmorgen the story of Captain Badenhausen. Two other shipwrecks with numerous deaths, the sinking of the Bremen three-masted barque "Johanne" in 1854 on its maiden voyage off the island of Spiekeroog and the sinking of the "Alliance" in 1860 close to Borkum, led to the founding of the Bremen Association for the Rescue of Shipwrecked Persons in 1863. Two years later, the German Society for the Rescue of Shipwrecked Persons was founded in Kiel. A passenger list from the archives of the Bremen Chamber of Commerce of the "Johanne" is online. And lo and behold – a few Hessians were also among those rescued, from Ober-kaufungen, from Hähnlein and from Lißberg. Valentin Henkel from Treysa survived. Misfortune did not dissuade him from emigrating. He traveled on the "Wilhelmine" to Baltimore. The body from Wilhelm Klüs from Raberts-hausen, a small village in today's district of Giessen, was found. Behind his name is written: "deceased, back to the homeland".

And the Sterns from Nieder-Ohmen? Hannah and Josef Stern worked hard to build a new life for themselves. Ruth has written an autobiographical book for young people about her life as a migrant child: "An Accidental American". Her grandmother and uncles from Ulmbach have found refuge in Africa. Her aunt Rifka Stern, her mentally handicapped aunt Toni, her uncle Meier, who was her father's brother, and his wife, her aunt Hedwig Stern, were murdered by the Nazis. Her cousins Hilda and Carola survived Auschwitz and came to the USA after the war. Hilda Stern Cohen's Holocaust poems were published after her death.[15]

Another Nieder-Ohmener, Siegfried Frank, had sailed from Hamburg to Cuba in 1939 on the "St. Louis", but the Cubans did not let the refugees ashore. They were also rejected in the United States and Canada. Captain Gustav Schröder succeeded in distributing his approximately 900 passengers to other countries and thus saving the lives of many of them. Siegfried Frank found refuge in the Netherlands, but was deported soon after the invasion of the Wehrmacht and murdered in Auschwitz shortly before his 35th birthday. Captain Schröder is commemorated today in Hamburg by a street, a park and a plaque at the Landungsbrücken. Not far from the place where the "St. Louis" had departed in May 1939. And the band played "Muss i denn"[16], a folk song from Swabia: "I have to, I have to go out to the city."

What special event does this wandering and soldier's song from the 19th century still remind us of? On October 1, 1958, a troop transport from the USA docked at the cruise quay in Bremerhaven. On the quay, the girls were screaming. And a couple of guys were screaming too. At 9:22 am, Elvis Presley went ashore, in uniform, his duffle bag over his shoulder. At Bremerhaven station, the train to Friedberg was waiting. Ten hours later, the 22-year-old was in his garrison, but days later he moved with his father, grandmother and two bodyguards to a hotel in Bad Nauheim. As a jeep driver of a reconnaissance squad, he

[15] See podcast part 6, chapter 6 of this book.

[16] In the podcast played by the Upper Hessian brass band „Herz 7".

traveled a lot in Hesse during his military service, and wherever he appeared, children, adolescents and adults gathered around him, photos[17] were taken and autographs were collected. At the end of his service in 1960, the King of Rock'n'Roll recorded "Muss i denn..." under the title "Wooden Heart". In his film "G. I. Blues" he languishes at Gretel, a hand puppet, in a Punch and Judy show, singing that song. Translated, it would go like this:

Must I, then

Must I, then, must I, then
leave this small town,
leave this small town,
and you, my dear, stay here!
When I'm back, when I'm back,
when I finally return, finally return,
I'll stay with you, my dear.

Only a few have returned, very few forever.

---

[17] See the photo made in Heimertshausen that is on display in the museum in Kirtorf, Upper Hesse – where you also find a room dedicated to the Social Revolutioneer Friedrich Ludwig Weidig who had not wanted to become a member of the Giessen Emigration Society (see podcast part 2) and had been reverend of Ober-Gleen when he was arrested by the police in 1835. The museum has its own website and is usually opend for several hours on Sundays. The Heimatverein Stadt Kirtorf is in charge.

A home far away from home

Emigration becomes immigration. Hessian contributions to American history of the 17th and 18th centuries

The New Colossus

Not like the brazen giant of Greek fame,
With conquering limbs astride from land to land;
Here at our sea-washed, sunset gates shall stand
A mighty woman with a torch, whose flame
Is the imprisoned lightning, and her name
Mother of Exiles. From her beacon-hand
Glows world-wide welcome; her mild eyes command
The air-bridged harbor that twin cities frame.
"Keep, ancient lands, your storied pomp!" cries she
With silent lips. "Give me your tired, your poor,
Your huddled masses yearning to breathe free,
The wretched refuse of your teeming shore.
Send these, the homeless, tempest-tost to me,
I lift my lamp beside the golden door!"[1]

When the poet Emma Lazarus wrote her poem "The New Colossus" in 1883, for the pedestal of the Statue of Liberty,

---

[1] From the sonett „The New Colossus" by Emma Lazarus, 1883. It starts with the lines: „Not like the brazen giant of Greek fame with conquering limbs astride from land to land here at our sea-washed, sunset gates shall stand a mighty woman with a torch, whose flame is the imprisoned lightning, and her name Mother of Exiles. From her beacon-hand glows world-wide welcome; her mild eyes command the air-bridged harbor that twin cities frame. „Keep, ancient lands, your storied pomp!" cries she with silent lips..."

the work was not yet finished. The Jewish sculptor Frédéric-Auguste Bartholdi from Colmar is still working on the monumental statue. For the six-metre-thick walls of the statue, cement is supplied from Amöneburg near Wiesbaden, made with lime from the Biebrich quarry. No less than 8000 barrels. "Liberty illuminates the world" is the original title of the statue in the shape of the Roman goddess Libertas, a gift from the French to the American people. When the Statue of Liberty was inaugurated on Bedloes Island in New York Harbor in 1886, several generations of Hessians and people from many other countries had already made a pilgrimage across the Atlantic. Life had written many migration stories during this time. In our podcast we tell some of them and describe how the legal situation has changed.

In 1660, Jacob Leisler, the penniless son of a pastor from Bockenheim, comes to America. He will get extremely rich, then become mayor of New York, will be hanged for alleged high treason and later rehabilitated.

In 1682, pietists join forces to form the "Frankfurter Land-Kompagnie", which wants to settle in North America. Nothing will come of it, but their negotiator, the Franconian lawyer Franz Pastorius, is present in 1683 when Krefeld Quakers and Mennonites found Germantown in Pennsylvania. And he has published a proclamation against human trafficking: "Although they are black, we cannot see that there would be a greater justification for keeping them as slaves than if we were dealing with whites. It is said that we should treat all people without distinction of sex, race, or skin color as one would like to be treated. (...)

There is freedom of belief here, (...) but there should also be freedom of the body."[2]

"Mir sai all Geschwisder" (We are all siblings), an Upper Hessian version by Monika Felsing, a coversong of the Klezmer song "Ale Brider" about the brotherhood and sisterhood of man. An audio from the benefit choir concert for "Reporters without Borders" at the Kulturtage Alsfeld in 2022.

In 1754 begins the French and Indian War. The French fight the British for nine years, both armies had Indian allies. One of the career officers in the service of the British, George Schneider from Fellingshausen near Giessen, keeps a diary about the war, as well as his first encounter with indigenous people in Albany: "The Wild or Indian Mans-persons are also well grown strong men, black-brown in color and, like the Moors or Tartarn, some have bent dog-noses. Then they cut off the earlobes so that they are only a little attached and weave a silver strand around them. In the nose they usually wear a ring of silver, or a piece of silver carved into a figure. Around the arms above the elbows, they wear a broad silver ribbon, in which the name of the nation and the acts of its heroes is engra-ved."[3]

In 1776, Americans write and sign the Declaration of Independence, which officially starts the Revolution. The document circulates, also in German. At this time, about

---

[2] Proclamation against Sclavery, April 18, 1688. In: Brandt. Bau deinen Altar auf fremder Erde, quoted as on the Krefeld website www.angekommen.com.
[3] Gräf, p. 127.

ten out of 100 inhabitants of the colonies are of German origin.

In 1777, the 57-year-old gingerbread baker Christoph Ludwig from Giessen who has seen the world is appointed chief baker of the Independence Army by Congress. Meanwhile, 12,000 men from Hesse-Kassel, who were leased to the colonial power by their sovereign, are fighting on the side of the British. Christoph Ludwig can't stand the thought, and he pities these soldiers. In the publication "Der Deutsche Pionier" (The German Pioneer) from October 1876, Ludwig is quoted: "Bring the Hessian prisoners of war to Philadelphia, show them our beautiful German churches, let them try our roast beef and show them our household goods, and them send them back to their fellowmen. And you will see how many of them will surrender."[4]

In 1781 the German Society is founded in Philadelphia, and three years later the one in New York.

In 1783, the War of Independence ends with the Treaty of Paris.

In 1790, the laws stipulate that immigrants could become naturalized after a minimum stay of two years.

In 1819 ship captains are told to keep lists of immigrants' names and submit them upon arrival in the U.S.

In 1823, the 21-year-old Wilhelm Bernbeck from Gleiberg doesn't finish his law studies in Giessen, emigrates to the

---

[4] Hessisches Auswandererbuch, pp. 138 f.

United States, and joins the Texas struggle for independence against Mexico in 1836. At about the same time,
his family in Germany connects with the Münch family.[5]

In 1837, Georg Münch from Niedergemünden, the
younger brother of Friedrich Münch of the Giessen
Emigration Society, and Charlotte Strack from Gleiberg,
a niece of Wilhelm Bernbeck and great-granddaughter
of the soldier George Schneider, who has returned to
Germany, married. Mr. and Mrs. Münch emigrate to
Missouri, where Georg and his brother Friedrich will found
one of the first wineries in the United States[6]. The year
1837 is a dark year in Hessian as well as in German history:
Friedrich Ludwig Weidig dies in Darmstadt prison where
he had been held for two years in isolation, without a trial.
The head of school from Butzbach and reverend of
Ober-Gleen has been so desperate that he committed
suicide. Other leaders of the Social Revolution also died
in this year or fled to America.

In the podcast, their memory is honored by the song "Ean
dene dongle Zaire" (In these dark times), written by
Monika Felsing, sung by a project choir in the benefit
concert for "Reporters without Borders" at the Alsfelder
Kulturtage in Alsfeld Germany in 2022 to the melody of
Giaccomo Puccini's "O mio babbino caro". The lyrics say:
In these dark days, when human rights didn't count, you
could read secretly how wonderful the world could be.
Once the police came and took Weidig away. And showed

---

[5] Gräf, pp. 138 f.
[6] Gräf , pp. 138 f.

no mercy and left without a word. Time stood still, dreams did die when freedom was murdered.

In 1843, 21-year-old Anna Margarethe Schmidt leaves her hometown of Haunetal-Kruspis in Hesse and marries Johann Heinrich Heinz, a native of Rhineland-Palatinate, in Pennsylvania. Her chutneys are so well received that her son Henry John founds a ketchup empire.

In 1845, Prince Carl von Solms-Braunfels becomes general commissioner of the "Association for the Protection of German Emigrants to Texas", founded by him and other aristocrats. He settles 300 Germans in Texas, which has recently belonged to Mexico, calls the place "New Braunfels" and returns to Hesse. Some know him by his nickname: Texas Carl.

In 1847, New York State establishes an immigration office. The Commissioners of Emigration are supposed to put a stop to the "immigrant runners", shady characters who rob immigrants of their belongings. In the same year, the widow Hannah Hecht from Langenschwarz in Hesse arrives in Baltimore with her sons Samuel Junior and Ruben. Samuel Hecht will make his way from peddler to owner of a large department store chain.

In 1849, 20-year-old Heinrich Lomb, a carpenter, from Burghaun goes to the United States. He takes a stake in an optician's shop that will later become famous with "Ray Ban" glasses.

In 1853 August Becker, a member of parliament from Hesse, flees to the United States. As a companion of Georg

Büchner, Friedrich Ludwig and Amalie Weidig, he has been imprisoned at a young age. After his amnesty, he goes into exile in Switzerland in 1839 and does not return to Giessen until 1848. He stands for election and becomes a member of the Second Chamber of the Estates for an Upper Hessian constituency. When the political opponents of the revolution turn back the clock, he leaves Germany again, this time for good. In the United States, August Becker first works in a circus, then until his death as an editor in Cincinnati, New York, Baltimore and Washington. During the Civil War, he becomes field chaplain in the Steuben Regiment.

In 1855, the former Castle Garden artillery position is converted into a receiving station for all those who had travelled on the tween deck.

In 1857, 18-year-old Adolph Busch from Kastel goes to the United States. After marrying Lilly Annheuser, the daughter of a beer brewer from the Palatinate, he advances the business with his ideas. He has a summer residence, Villa Lilly, built in Hesse, near his hometown. And there he will also die. His body returns to the United States.

In 1858, Johann Georg Will from Launsbach emigrates to the United States. What happened to him is told in an open-air museum, the Hessenpark, not far from Frankfurt.

In 1859, Friedrich Münch publishes Der Staat Missouri, geschildert mit besonderer Rücksicht auf teutsche Einwanderung“ in New York. The state of Missouri, described with particular regard to German immigration.

Emigrants in a newspaper illustration from the 19th century.

In 1862, with the Homestead Act, the United States government offers land in certain areas to all settlers, if they agree to cultivate it for at least five years.[7]

In 1866, 15-year-old Christoph J. Tebbens from Leer emigrates with his family from Bremerhaven to New York on the sailing ship "Shakespeare". His memoirs can be read on the website of the Heimatmuseum Leer.

Panis Angelicus (song, piano). Gabriele Gonder Carey, an American citizen born in Hamburg with roots in Hesse, has once recorded the song Panis Angelicus for a project of the historical society Lastoria, Bremen. In 1872, composer César Franck had set the hymn of Thomas of Aquin from the Middle Ages into music. The Lyrics in free translation: "The bread of the angels becomes the bread of human beings. The bread from heaven turns imagination into figure. How wonderful that its! The poor, devoted servant eats the lord. We pray to you, triune, unique god. Visit us, as we adore you. Lead us on your path to the light you are living in. Amen." Gabriele, born in 1954, migrated as a child. Her father and her mother went with her to Southern California in 1961. The family's story has been told in the first part of our podcast.

In 1875, the first laws are passed to exclude groups. From now on, convicts and prostitutes are no longer allowed to immigrate to America. And Friedrich Münch's guide book for Missouri is published again, this time in Bremen, under the title "Der Staat Missouri. Ein Handbuch für

---

[7] Georg Asmus, Hessisches Auswandererbuch, p. 56.

deutsche Auswanderer". The State of Missouri. A hand-book for German emigrants.

In 1882, the Immigration Act limits, among other things, immigration from China. Previously, Chinese have been met with hostility in California, and for the next ten years no more Chinese will be allowed to immigrate, and no Chinese will be naturalized. Former convicts and the mentally handicapped are excluded from entering the United States, and later anarchists from Tsarist Russia and other countries, epileptics, tuberculosis sufferers and professional beggars are also blacklisted, the poorest of the poor anyway. Anyone who threatens to become a burden on the American state is not allowed to immigrate. An immigration tax is levied.

In 1883, the German Society of the City of New York publishes a free "Rathgeber für deutsche Einwanderer" (Advice for German Immigrants), including a city map for the southern part of New York, which at this time is considered the "third largest German city in the world" after Berlin and Vienna. The book also includes a floor plan of Castle Garden and the names of the European correspondents for money transactions, in Hesse, for example, in Kassel, Darmstadt and Frankfurt am Main.

In 1887, two trade unionists from Hesse and one from Bremen are hanged in Chicago. George Engel from Kassel and August Spies from Friedewald near Bad Hersfeld had organized a strike lasting several days together with other labour leaders for better working conditions on the First of May, the day on which jobs were traditionally changed or employment contracts extended in the U.S.[*] Flyers in English and German are distributed, for a mass rally on the haymarket. During the rally a bomb had been thrown into the crowd. Twelve people died on the spot, among them a policeman, and others died in hospital. Though there was no evidence who had thrown the bomb, August Spies, George Engel, Albert Parsons and Adolph Fischer were held responsible and sentenced to death. "You can't live as an animal for eternity", August Spies had said on the haymarket. And to those who had sentenced him to death: "Time will come when our silence is more powerful than the voices you suffocate today!" The 29-year-old Adolph Fischer, a type setter from Bremen, anarchist and father of three children is said to have cried out before he was hanged: "Hurrah for anarchy! This is the happiest moment of my life!" In consequence of these events the First of May is declared to be Labor Day.

Several decades later, women who worked on the rice fields in Northern Italy used to sing a protest song: "Ciao, bella, ciao!" In the podcast there is an Upper Hessian version: "Ciao, Lina, ciao", written and sung by Monika Felsing tells the story of someone who is leaving his home country, hoping for a better life and for worker's and women's rights.

In 1891, the Office of Immigration is established as a division of the United States Treasury.

---

[*] See Wikipedia, https://www.museum-friedewald.de, https://www.documental4.de/de/artists/21991/august-spies. A letter from Parsons is on https://historymatters.gmu.edu. The book of Lucy Parsons is quoted there.

In the light of Lady Liberty's Torch

How immigrants experienced their arrival on Ellis Island

Welcome to the lobby of the United States, on the island of tears and American Dreams!

In 1892, Ellis Island is opened as a collection point for immigrants outside the New York city area because Castle Garden has been overloaded. The first emigrant to be registered is a 15-year-old Irish woman: Annie Moore receives a gold coin worth ten dollars as welcome money. In the German Emigration Center in Bremerhaven[1], the individual stations that third-class passengers have to pass through on Ellis Island are restructured.

For poor emigrants like Annie Moore[2], entering Ellis Island might be the start of a new, a better life. But there are also Europeans traveling to the U.S. with a return ticket, early, carefree tourists, even groups on guided round trips, keeping diaries and taking photos.

[1] See https://dah-bremerhaven.de.

[2] Annie Moore (1874-1924) was from Queenstown (Cobh/County: Cork) where later, in 1912, the "Titanic" would wait for the last passengers. There is a statue in Cobh and one in Ellis Island of her with her younger brothers whom she cared for. Their parents were in Manhattan, already, living there since 1888. Annie married a catholic German, Joseph Augustus Schayer (1876-1960). Her husband was the son of a German immigrant from Munich/Bavaria, a salesman who worked at the fish market. Annie gave birth to eleven children, lost five of them before they were three years old. Her grave is in Calvary Cemetery, Queens. The software program "Annie" is named after her, a program that was "developed at Worcester Polytechnic Institute in Massachusetts, Lund University in Sweden, and the University of Oxford in Britain which uses a 'matching algorithm' to allocate refugees with no ties to the host country to their new homes" (Wikipedia). See also https://www.theatlantic.com and findeagrave.com where there are also photos of Annie.

121

In 1893, Baedecker launched an American guide, and the German tour operator Carl Stangen offers the first package tour to the United States. The fast steamer "Saale" carries 57 wealthy travelers to America, mostly men, but also some women, from Bremerhaven to New York. One of the tourists, 26-year-old Belgian William Davignon, has his camera with him. The photos from his album "Une voyage aux Etats-Unis 1893" can be admired on the website of the Leibniz Institute for Regional Geography: There is Stangen's Party, as the group calls itself, on board the "Saale" and at Niagara Falls, and views of New York and San Francisco, Indians on the track, an opium cave in China Town, Yosemite Park and other national parks and of course the World's Fair in Chicago³.

The German writer Heinrich Lemcke seems to know Ellis Island and Castle Garden like the back of his hand. In 1883 he published the book "Souvenir to the Atlantic Ocean for Instruction and Entertainment for Travelers to America". And in 1896 his book on North America has just been published in Leipzig: "Canada, the country and its people. A guide and geographical handbook, containing a description of Canada with special reference to its economic conditions, as well as its settlement and colonization". In it, he also described the arrival at the port of New York. Since 1883, the superintendent of the pier has been Edmund Badenhausen, a captain from Melsungen in Hesse, of whom we have already heard.

In an article, Heinrich Lemcke describes the arrival of an overseas ship: "As soon as the ship approaches the port

³ Search with „Stangen's Party" on https://leibniz-ifl.de.

and lands at Staten Island, the quarantine doctor of the State of New York appears on board to subject all tween deck passengers to an examination of their state of health, regardless of the ship's doctor's certificate. This is done in such a way that all passengers on deck pass in front of the doctor and he tries to judge according to the appearance of the individual persons whether someone shows symptoms of illness: In such a case, the whole ship (if the disease is contagious) is placed in quarantine. From Staten Island, the ship reaches its landing site, called the pier, in New York or Hoboken, opposite the former cosmopolitan city, in an hour's journey. The cabin passengers leave the ship here along with all their luggage."[4]

And while the cabin passengers may follow Lemcke's advice and take a room in the hotel "Hamburger und Bremer Haus" at the foot of the third alley in Hoboken after customs control, the passengers from the cheaper seats still have one stop ahead of them: "The tweendeck passengers and their luggage are transported by the large

---

[4] Lemcke is quoted in this podcast part from his article about the arrival in the U.S. in the „Gartenlaube" from 1897, translated by Monika Felsing with the help of Susan Eldridge and Al. See also „The Devil's Isle (Knauf/Moreno, Leaving Home, p. 104, Bibliographie part I). In this article from 1910 under the title „Answers" the journalists describes the scenery as follows: „Before being officially recieved on American soil, immigrants to New York are taken over to Ellis Island. When the vessel arrives alongside the liner, loud orders are given to the immigrants: *All form in line for the shore! Close up! Step this way with your green health-cards handy! Bring all your hand baggage with you!* On Ellis Island, a specialist examines everyone for trachoma, „folding back each eyelid in a very rough manner". Next, the immigrants are individually chalked. The journalist is, as he realises, "one of fifty white, black, red and yellow immigrants". And: "*Strip!* Comes the order. Take everything off and line up as you were born. I protest. I am a Britisher. *No matter!* comes the answer. Line up naked like the rest! We strip one by one, pass up for inspection. I am tested and told to *Cough! Cough again!* And then, as something is written on my paper, to *Pass along and dress! Take this report with you!*"

steamer in small river vessels, specially prepared for the transport of the arrivals now called "immigrants" in the territory of the New World, directly to Castle Garden, the state landing depot for immigrants in New York", Heinrich Lemcke wrote. "This large immigration depot is a model institution of its own kind."

And so, the 15-year-old Christoph Tebbens from East Frisia in Northern Germany experiences his arrival in 1866: "New York! Castle Garden! With my extensive knowledge of the English language, I had nothing more important to do than to translate this name into German for my dear parents and all those who wanted to hear it: Castle – Schloss, Garden – Garten, i.e., Schlossgarten. That's right, said Uncle Gerhard, but my father smiled. Of course, the garden, consisting of a few lawns with some undergrowth, seemed inviting enough to us after the long sea voyage. But the building, the "castle"! An old, dilapidated looking, wooden round castle, but very spacious."[5]

Heinrich Lemcke is familiar with the formalities that have to be completed in the United States even before arrival: "In order to facilitate control, the steamship companies must keep 'manifestos' which answer twenty different questions concerning immigrants. These certificates shall state the age, sex, marital status, nationality, previous place of residence and destination of the immigrants, whether the person concerned can read and write, whether he is in possession of a transit rail ticket to his American destination, whether he has paid for the passage from his own resources or at whose expense he has

_____
[5] See above, website of Heimatmuseum Leer.

Immigrants in a newspaper illustration from the 19th century.

travelled. whether he is in possession of money, whether and to which relatives he travels, whether he is healthy or afflicted with physical infirmities, and so on. The manifesto must be sworn by the captain and the physician of the ship in question before a U.S. consul abroad before commencing the voyage and shall form the basis for the examination of immigrants at the U.S. landing depot."

Those who have passed all the checks in Castle Garden wait in the inner rotunda of the building until they continue. An official reads out the names of those to whom a letter or money has been sent, or who are picked up by relatives or acquaintances. Against receipt. "This prevents newcomers, especially women and young girls, from falling into bad hands", Heinrich Lemcke reports.

And that's how the Tebbens family experiences it in 1866: "The many immigrants ran back and forth, not knowing what to do first. We settled down on our luggage. The heads of families or individuals were now interrogated in turn by the customs officers, and officials of the German society, about their belongings and where they came from and where they were going. They were then given the best possible advice, and one by one they departed. Some were picked up by relatives, but most were taken in tow by hotel agents, known as "runners" in this country. These were very rubbed fellows, and it was not easy to get out of their hands one whom they wanted to maneuver to their respective inn."

In Castle Garden, the newcomers are still courted by the hotel agents decades later. Who should they go with?

Who is reputable? Heinrich Lemcke has his own suggestions for his readership: "For all those who want to stay in New York for a few more days, there is an opportunity to make a suitable choice among the agents of concessioned inns who suddenly storm into the rotunda under the reputation of "boarding houses". I have visited all the immigrant Logis houses in New York in the interest of immigrants and can highly recommend the following lodging houses..."

... and German names follow. These are the times when New York hotels are still called "Hôtel Grütli" or "Württemberger Hof", "Hammers Hôtel", "Emigranten-Haus" or "Stuttgarter Hof" and you still have to pay one to one and a half dollars for an overnight stay. And as far as other costs are concerned... "...tipping is not customary in the United States of America and Canada and is therefore never given or requested", Heinrich Lemcke has learned. "The transport of people and luggage from Castle Garden to the station, the weighing of luggage et cetera is also free of charge, under the control of the responsible officer."

And in 1897, the 53-year-old Heinrich Lemcke came to Ellis Island to report on the innovations for the gazebo. He has taken the free steamboat that connects Manhattan with Ellis Island as a ferry and is allowed to roam freely on the seven-and-a-half-acre island. Immigration Commissioner Dr. Joseph Senner, a Democrat, receives him, and Lemcke is suitably impressed. The main building is 160 meters long and 50 meters wide, the basement houses the baggage magazine, the second floor houses the registration hall and the offices. There is also a hospital, a machine house, and various sheds.

"At first, I positioned myself in the large registration hall in such a way that I could best overlook the 'invasion' of immigrants from the Hamburg mail steamer 'Pennsylvania'. Next to me were some American women dressed in silk and velvet, who might have a special interest in the visit to Ellis Island", Heinrich Lemcke reports. "In one room we see a German family that forms almost an entire family tree. There are fifteen people – that's what counts! There, in a corner, we see a very young, pretty girl, an orphan, scarcely sixteen years old, who made the journey across the ocean alone; here we see a group of emaciated men, who visibly drove misery out of their homeland; there, a mother seeks to satisfy the hunger of a crying infant; here, an expert on the country gives his ship's friends, all young, downy-bearded men, a lecture on the American art of getting rich. – And now even the confusion of languages! The many dialects of this international society!"

Everyone has to line up at one of the four registration slots. The documents are examined, including the ship's manifests, and questions are asked. The whole thing takes three to seven hours. Those who have successfully survived it are picked up by relatives or acquaintances or wait at the landing depot until the train heads west.

"What is one and one?", asked one of the immigration officers who sit on high chairs and have interpreters by their side. "Do you have a job? Do you have any diseases? Do you have relatives or acquaintances with whom you will be staying? Have you ever been to the United States?

Have you ever been in prison or in an almshouse? What race do they belong to? Are you a polygamist? Do you have any money with you, at least $50? What do you want in the United States? Do you clean stairs from top to bottom or from bottom to top? Are you an anarchist? Are you planning to assassinate the President of the United States of America?"

Illiterate, sick, and criminals, or those who could be, are rejected; parents have to decide whether to send their sick child back on their own. As soon as they climb the 50 steps to the registration room, the new arrivals are observed by doctors: Does anyone have heart problems or perhaps a stiff leg? Two out of a hundred people are rejected, about 100 to 120 each day. Over the course of six decades, there are about 250,000 who are not allowed to enter the country for medical, political, or other reasons. 300 desperate people are said to have taken their own lives. Heinrich Lemcke has the impression that the rejected people who are waiting for their deportation lack nothing.

"The immigrants declared ineligible for landing by this board will receive extremely humane treatment on Ellis Island until they are transported back to Europe", Heinrich Lemcke reports. "The food for these poor is strong, tasty, and plentiful. The bedrooms and washrooms are of the most meticulous cleanliness."
And that is Senner's merit.

In his article of 1897, Heinrich Lemcke repeated almost verbatim at the beginning of his report on Ellis Island what he had reported in May 1886 in the "Husumer Wochen-blatt" about the check-in in Castle Garden – about the arrival of 1200 women, men, and children from the tween deck of the "Rugia". Whether fantasy was also involved can no longer be verified. But let's let him tell: "At a given bell signal, the door to the registration hall suddenly opened, and now a swarm of several hundred immigrants moved into the giant hall. In terms of nationality, most of them were Germans, but there were also many Austrians, Hungarians, Russians, Swiss, Swedes, Norwegians, and Danes. In single file, with boxes, crates and bundles, old junk, and ancestral household goods, often packed with infants, they passed by, subjected to criticism by doctors, and were then distributed into rooms separated by wire bars for thirty people each. A peculiar sight, this whole scenery! The younger ones, especially the girls, have dressed themselves up festively, the dear vanity of the fair youth allows them no other way than to set foot on the soil of the New World. The older generation of immi-grants, however, follows a different principle. 'It's just good enough for the trip' seems to be the guiding idea here."

Whoever can answer the questions to the satisfaction of the officials is allowed to go ashore. Those who do not are subjected to a special interrogation in a separate department and are brought before the Board of Special Inquiry, a court of inquiry consisting of four inspectors and a secretary. In 1886 alone, 43,645 people had to face the Board of Special Inquiry. Anyone who fails has to wait in the landing depot for a steamship company to depart, and is brought back to Europe at the expense of the shipping company like an unwanted postal package:

acceptance refused. In 1886, 2,374 people were sent back, mainly destitute people from Italy, Hungary, Austria, Russia, England, and Ireland. Many of them can neither read nor write. For Heinrich Lemcke, the interrogations of this Board of Special Inquiry were "the most interesting spectacle" that could be enjoyed on Ellis Island. If you are not interrogated yourself.

"Righteous people who are oppressed by misery through no fault of their own, failed existences brought down by their own fault, fate juxtaposes here", Heinrich Lemcke reports. "A Russian Jew who claims to have been in America for two years is subjected to a harsh inter-rogation. He speaks a little broken English. The chairman asks him: "What were you here in America?" And the Russian Jew answers: "Tailor!" The Judge wants to know: „Have you never been begging here?"

"The Russian doesn't know the word begging, and unable to answer, he turns to the interpreter for assistance. "Thou shalt say whether thou hast scrounged when thou hast been in America", says the man, and the Russian Jew cries out: "God the righteous shall preserve me when I have scrounged!"

"And since a fellow countryman known to him, resident in New York, has arrived, who undertakes to the Immigration Commission to guarantee that the new-comer will not be a burden on the public care of the poor, he is allowed to land", Heinrich Lemcke goes on. "Another Russian, a young farmer, is not as happy as his predecessor. He is a healthy, strong young man, who is able to work hard, but has only 15 cents of cash with him, so that, according to the laws of the country, this young, faithful blood must be transported back to Russia. If it is not possible to find someone in the next few days who will engage the young man and take him with him."

The whole thing resembles a play, a melodrama with or without a happy ending: "An Italian woman, a widow with three small children and a nineteen-year-old son, explains to the Board that although they are all destitute, her son is working and wants to be their breadwinner. The members of the Board look at each other in disbelief and shake their heads. But the young man knows how to make such a favorable impression on the Board through his unvarnished clarification of the facts that, especially since compatriots also vouch for the immigrants, they do not deny the family entry into the New World."

It goes on. "Now an elderly German, who is in his fifties and must have been shipwrecked in his life, comes forward and confesses that he is impoverished and that his family, wife and children, are still in Germany. A German-American family he knows wants to find him work. The wife of a German innkeeper from New York is already stepping forward: "We know the man and want to employ him as a dishwasher and servant in our dining room." And a Member of the Board requires: 'And if the man does not work to your satisfaction? What then?' The Innkeeper's wife doesn't hesitate: 'Then we will send him home at our expense.'"

"This man was also granted landing", Heinrich Lemcke writes. "How will he fare in his new position? Again, a completely impoverished man, a shoemaker from Russia,

Castle Garden and New York in the "Buch der Erfindungen" .

New York aus der Vogelschau.

is called before the Board of Special Inquiry. (...) He says that he has a brother in America who has been living in Brooklyn for a long time. But the brother hasn't shown up. 'Back to Russia, if your brother doesn't come to guarantee you,' is the Board of Special Inquiry's decision. Dejected, the poor man staggers to a bench and sits down on it. But only for a moment. Suddenly, he hears a well-known voice calling his name. It is the brother who has just come. An outcry when they both see and recognize each other! They hug and tears of joy run from their cheeks. Everyone and every etiquette are forgotten, the spectators, even the members of the Board are moved and there is a longer pause. Thankfully, the brother is able to give the Board sufficient guarantee that the immigrant will not be a burden on the public care of the poor, and both then stroll away with great pleasure."

Klezmer Improvisation, played by Yale Strom (San Diego) and others in a workshop, Villa Ichon, Bremen, 2019.

A few decades later, Jewish Europeans and other victims of Nazi persecution have no chance of seeking safety in the United States without a guarantee. Quotas and internal instructions to the responsible officials ensure that the number is much lower than originally planned. Many hope in vain for a visa, such as Betty Baer nee Sondheim from Ober-Gleen and her son Alfred, who wanted to flee from Amsterdam to the United States and were murdered by the Nazis. Betty's siblings Bertha and Siegmund Sondheim, her sister-in-law Jettchen, her nieces Addi and Rita and her nephew Herbert, the Sterns from Nieder-

Ohmen and the Sterns from Diez an der Lahn can be saved.* After the Kristallnacht, the pogrom in 1938, relatives vouched for them and set money as security for the next few years. Siegmund Sondheim is so weakened as a result of his imprisonment in the Dachau concentration camp that he first has to go to hospital after arriving in New York. The family is still allowed to enter the country.

Back in 1897, Heinrich Lemcke also visited the hospital on the island. 350 children will be born here over the decades, 3,500 patients will die, and the contagiously ill will be separated from their relatives. "Soon I was standing in front of the chief physician of the hospital, invited by him to take a seat with a courteous 'please'", Heinrich Lemcke writes. "As I learned from him, the number of sick people in the last year amounted to 1717 persons, i.e., approximately one-half per cent of all immigrants, whose total number in 1896 was 263,709 persons. Of the sick, 40 people died, but 10 children also saw the light of day here. The total number of catering days was 14,503. A tour of the rooms of the hospital made me see everywhere the most meticulous cleanliness and the excellent care that the sick find here."

And he goes to the Ellis Island Bureau of Statistics to do some research. According to Heinrich Lemcke, "of the 263,709 immigrants who landed, 66,445 were from Italy, Austria-Hungary 52,085, Russia 39,859, England 38,226,

---

* The books of the oral history project about Ober-Gleen, written by Monika Felsing, like "Himmel un Höll" and the audio book "Yiddish Life", but also the memorial book "Bettys Nachbarn. Betty's buren" about exile in Amsterdam 1933-1945, and the book "The Gate" written by Ruth Stern Glass Earnest whose mother was from Ober-Gleen.

Germany 24,230, Sweden 16,379, Norway 6599, Denmark 2820, Portugal 2476, Holland 1465, Switzerland 2253, Turkey 4252. The German immigrants brought with them the largest percentage of money and made up the smallest percentage among the 'illiterates'."

And what about the financing of Ellis Island? "Since the shipping companies that land immigrants in the United States have to pay a bounty of one dollar for each, which goes into the government's 'Immigrant Fund,' this tax is not only sufficient to cover all the expenses for the maintenance of the institutions, but also to generate a considerable surplus every year", Heinrich Lemcke has been told. As a visitor, he can leave the island whenever he pleases. He's not the only one looking for something.

"Fully satisfied with the impressions gained on Ellis Island, I turned to go to the ferry", Heinrich Lemcke writes. "On the way there, I met the elegant American women again, who had previously watched the spectacle with me in the registration room. A young, pretty girl, a German, in a simple calico suit, stood in front of them. The father and mother of the young immigrant woman, apparently belonging to the peasantry, next to her. 'Well, you'll leave your daughter to me as a maid? She's supposed to have a good time! I'll pay her $14 a month!', said one of the ladies. And the father: 'Mother, what do you think?' The mother stutters: "It should be fine with me." Tears ran softly from her cheek. And the daughter? She agreed. After all, she had come to America to earn lots and lots of money. A few moments later and the young girl will drive away with the elegant ladies, while her parents will rush west on a railroad train to settle there as farmers on the prairie. Will it be a breakup forever?"

An outcry tears him out of his thoughts: "Mien Söhn, o mien Söhn!" Heinrich Lemcke recalls the scene: "I looked and saw an old mother weeping and sobbing on the neck of a handsome young man. The situation was easily explained. It was a young German who had emigrated several years ago and who, having achieved prosperity through work, had now had his elderly parents join him. Here, on Ellis Island, they saw each other for the first time in many years. The joy of the reunion was too great for the mother, she had to rejoice and weep at the breast of her son at the same time."

It's evening, and he's taking the ferry to Manhattan. "When I landed at Battery Park in New York, I saw all sorts of suspicious figures, peasant catchers, who, like a pack, follow the ignorant immigrant at every turn during his appearance from Ellis Island and try to rob them of their belongings. True gallows birds!", he observes and tries to put himself in the shoes of the people he met on Ellis Island. "What a painful experience such an immigrant often has to go through before he has completely found his way in the New World! Every newcomer feels inclined to comparisons between the newly chosen and the motherland, the beginning is usually very difficult, the memories of youth rise in the distance to ideal height! Soon the poor man finds himself in that state of illness that in earlier times, when travel was still limited to a few, was attributed to the Swiss as hereditary. Homesickness has broken out in full force in him and only sooner or later gives way to the one who finds success or happiness in the New World."

Klezmer Improvisation, from a workshop lead by Klezmer artist Yale Strom (San Diego) in the Villa Ichon, Bremen, Germany, in 2019.

Welcome Or Not Welcome?
A fearful question

How the conditions of immigration to the United States have changed since the early 20th Century

Yes, they are coming, the tired, the poor, the huddled masses who long to breathe free. Are the wretched ones rejected on the besieged shores of North America? Will they, the homeless people driven by the storm, be sent back to Europe like the 937 passengers on the Hapag ship "St. Louis"? Jewish refugees like Siegfried Frank from Nieder-Ohmen, whom the Nazis would then murder in Auschwitz? Lady Liberty holds her lamp high next to the golden door. But immigration policy will be tightened over the next few decades.

In 1911, the Dillingham Commission publishes its report on the social impact of immigration. It has concluded that those who immigrated to the United States after 1890 pose a danger to society in the United States, and distinguishes between old and new immigration.

In 1917, the first reading and writing tests are held for those wishing to enter the country.

In 1921 The Immigration Act limits annual immigration to 350,000 people and introduces quotas for nationalities.

In 1924, annual immigration was limited to 165,000 people.

In 1927 there are only 150,000. The quota for nationalities will also be redefined. The number of immigrants in a nation may be two percent of the number of its compatriots from the 1920 census. This law remains in force until 1965 and, above all, reduces the number of immigrants from Africa and Asia.

In 1929, during the Great Depression, a new quota is set. 70 percent of the 150,000 people who are allowed to immigrate have to be from northern and western Europe, the rest from southern and eastern Europe.

Dona Dona, Klezmer, lyrics in Upper Hessian dialect.[1]

In 1933, only 23,068 people are allowed to immigrate. After the Nazis come to power, there is a run on the US consulates. But only a few visas are issued.

In April 1934, Norbert Goldenberg, born in Kestrich, Upper Hesse, emigrates to the U.S. Because of Nazi laws, he has lost his job as an assistant at the University Clinic for Internal Medicine of Frankfurt/Main and his approbation as a physician. Almost right away he is appointed as Vice-President of the German-Jewish Club and "The Aufbau", a German-Jewish newspaper. Three decades later, he will be its President and publisher. At the "Aufbau", he meets his future wife, Lilo Lamm, a refugee from Berlin, daughter of Leopold Lamm from Homberg/Ohm. She is working as a secretary and will write essays about her family all her life. As soon as possible,

---

[1] Audio from a benefit concert for "Reporters without Borders" at the Kulturtage Alsfeld in 2022.

Norbert Goldenberg works as a physician again. In 1936, he passes his American medical examination and works in a hospital before opening an office and private practice in Washington Heights, "Frankfurt on the Hudson", a home away from home for many German emigrants.[2]

Saa, kennsde mech? Tell me, do you know me or don't you? Out of sight, out of mind? An Upper Hessian version of Auld Lang Syne.[3]

In 1937, the eleven-year-old Kurt Wilhelm Freund from Nuremberg and his parents cross the Atlantic. His mother Paula Gruenstein Freund from Miltenberg has a knowledge that will help the family to survive. She has bribed a baker at the famous Häberlein-Metzger Lebkuchen manufactory to give her the secret recipe. During WWII, she bakes and sells "Paulas Celebrated Lebkuchen". There are advertisings in the "Aufbau", and the New York Herald Tribune publishes about her Nürnberger Elisen Lebkuchen startup in December 1939: "Germany ousted Paula, so she mastered a baker's art". And she is quoted: "Nazis couldn't stop anyone from taking something away in the head." William Curt Freund as her son calls himself after getting American citizenship, becomes chief economist of the New York stock Exchange and marries the photographer Irmgard (Judith) Steinberger, born in Alsfeld in 1920. Her family had fled to Haifa in August 1933, and she came to

---

[2] Lilo Goldenberg Family Collection on https://archives.cjh.org. See as well https://www.lbi.org/de/collections/periodicals/aufbau, https://www.alemannia-judaica.de/kestrich_synagoge.htm and publications concerning the "Aufbau", as on Wikipedia.
[3] An audio from a singing workshop with Monika Felsing in the former Synagogue of Ober-Gleen, recorded in 2019.

the U.S. after the war. Daughter Nancy is married to Jeffrey Heller, a human rights activist, writer and lawyer, specialized in Immigration Law. He "has dedicated his life to combating prejudice and raising awareness about refugees and migrants in the United States", as can be read on the website of Human Rights First.[4]

Klezmer Improvisation, from a workshop lead by Klezmer artist Yale Strom (San Diego) in the Villa Ichon, Bremen, Germany, in 2019.

Dina Gardner, née Nussbaum from Ulmbach, had emigrated to the United States with her sister Regina before the First World War. In 1939, the widow vouched for the family of her niece Hanna. Like many other patriotic German Jews, the Sterns had hesitated to leave their hometown, their homeland and Europe. After the pogrom night of November 1938, the socalled "Kristallnacht", followed by the internment of ten thousands of Jewish men in concentration camps like Dachau and Buchenwald, it becomes crystal clear that Jews are in danger when Nazis are in power, and that the only rescue is to leave the country or, better, the continent. Like many Jews who fled from Eastern Europe after the pogroms in the late 19th century, Joseph and Hanna Stern from Nieder-Ohmen in Upper Hesse disembark from the "Deutschland" in New York with their five-year-old daughter. Ruth Stern Gasten has written about it in her childhood autobiography "An Accidental American".

---

[4] See the „Aufbau" online and New York Herald Tribune, December 1939, and the website of Human Rights First. The author of this book had met Nancy and Jeffrey Heller in Alsfeld, Upper Hesse, and also had the opportunity to speak with William Curt Freund once during a video call with his family.

Herbert Sondheim and his widowed mother Jettchen.

Ruth Stern Gasten: "We were back on solid ground and were led to the immigration offices. My mother had all the papers firmly in her hand. It was our turn. She handed everything over to a tall, thin, middle-aged man who wore a uniform. I wondered if most adults in the world wore uniforms. He carefully reviewed the information and said: "So! You are headed for Chicago, eh?" My mother heard "Chicago" and nodded, even though she had no idea what he wanted to know. After we finished with him, we had to go to the doctor to make sure we didn't have any serious illnesses. We didn't. And then we were outside, where thousands of eyes seemed to scan each and every one of us, looking for relatives. I don't know how my uncle Albert found us, but he found us. „Willkommen in Amerika, Joseph, Hanna und Ruthchen!"

Someone spoke to us in German. We turned around, and there he was – a short, round, almost bald man in a striped suit: Albert Stern, Daddy's youngest brother. Uncle Albert was an accountant and had been in New York for about ten years. He quickly waved for one of the many waiting taxis."

Family Sondheim from Ober-Gleen in Upper Hesse also fled to the United States. In 1939 Siegmund and Jette Sondheim, their children Addi, Herbert, and Rita and Siegmund's sister Berta went on board a ship. Robin Smolen née Sondheim who belongs to the first generation in New York tells the story of her family.[5]

---

[5] As documented as audio and text in the oral history project about Ober-Gleen and in the audio book "Yiddish Leben". The author is in contact with Robin Smolen.

Beatrice and Herbert Sondheim at their wedding.

"In 1939, my father, Herbert Sondheim, Daddy, was not yet twelve years old when he and his immediate family fled Germany and Hitler's persecution of the Jews", Robin Smolen nee Sondheim says. "They had to leave their home in Ober-Gleen and most of their possessions to escape to the safety of America. Upon arrival at Ellis Island, they settled in Washington Heights, a neighborhood in New York City with a big German Jewish community. Daddy had many relatives already living there who had previously arrived in NY from Germany. They lived with Aunts and Uncles at first before renting their own apartment. It was nice having family there since Daddy and his parents and siblings spoke no English and had to start over again in this new country. Everyone lived near each other, went to Synagogue together, took walks together and met for cake and coffee in the evenings. Family, friends and socializing, was important to them in Germany and continued to be even more so in New York. In New York City my grandfather became a merchant while my grandmother worked in a millinery factory making women's hats. My Aunt Addi who was older worked in an office and Daddy and his little sister Rita went to school. Daddy spoke no English and had to learn quickly to catch up. He was determined and became an excellent student."

Like many men of German descent or migrants born in Germany, Herbert Sondheim served the U.S. Army.

"When Daddy turned 18 in 1945 he was drafted into the army", says his daughter. "Feeling very grateful to be given the opportunity to start a new life in the U.S., Daddy proudly served his new country. He was a topographical surveyor, creating maps for the army. He served with honor and pride. When he was 19, his father died and he was honorably discharged to go home and support his family. Daddy worked full time during the day to support his family and attended College full time at night. He graduated with a degree in Accounting. While in college, Daddy began working at an international shipping company. Daddy started as a bookkeeper, worked his way up to Accountant, Treasurer and was then offered ownership of the company, which he accepted. He had a most exciting experience, owning large freight vessels, acting as agent for shippers and dealing with many governments, learning the ins and outs of the shipping business and traveling all over the world. He became well known and highly respected in the industry and also acted as a lead arbitrator for the Maritime Society."

He was a family man by then, as he had married at a young age and founded a family. It was love at first sight.

"Daddy met my mom - Beatrice or Beatie or Bea as he called her - and the love of his life at a dance in Manhattan when he was 23", Robin Smolen knows. "He saw a beautiful blonde come out of the rest room with her girl friends and bet his friends that he would get her to dance with him. She did and they were married in 1952. They rented an apartment in Washington Heights near his mother and made a happy life there. My two sisters were born shortly after and my parents decided it was time to buy a house in the suburbs. They bought a house in 1960 and four years later I was born. Daddy and Mom raised us with love and pride, instilling the values important to them. My sisters and I had a happy childhood filled with love and laughter and fun and adventures."

Back in the Seventies*, Herbert Sondheim had explained German proverbs and even a joke on Antisemites to one of his sons-in-law. The recording has stood the test of time. In the background, his wife, Beatrice Sondheim and one or two children are to be heard. To get the joke with the policeman, one has to keep in mind that many Jews are circumcised and that men did not wear their watch around the wrist as in former times.

Herbert Sondheim: „And so it was. Back in Germany, in 1935, a policeman in Frankfurt at the train station, on the platform, said to a fella: ‚Hey, Jew, what time is it?' And the jew turned around and answered: ‚Now that you could look through my pants, you can also look through my vest pocket!'"
Son-in-law: „How was that in German?"
Herbert Sondheim: „We said: ‚Jude, wie viel Uhr ist es?' ‚Du hast mir durch die Hose geguckt, jetzt schau mir durch die Westentasche!'"

And he goes on.

Herbert Sondheim: „Der Apfel fällt nicht weit vom Baum. Means, the apple doesn't fall far from the tree. If the egg is smarter than the chicken, that doesn't do any good. Wenn das Ei *geschaider* is (gescheiter ist) wie ein Huhn, das tut kein' gut. A thought that just came to mind

---

* The recording, a tape, is from the Seventies. We have tried to cancel the side noises of the tape recorder.

Robin Smolen nee Sondheim on the Jewish cemetery of Angenrod in 2019.

is: Wenn ich mir was wünschen dürfte, käm ich in Verlegenheit. If I could... I translate it: If I could wish myself something, I would be embarrassed, for I have everything and I can't think for anything that I could wish for myself."

The original, one of Marlene Dietrich's songs, goes on like this: "...what I should wish for, a good or a bad time." And then, Herbert Sondheim recalled his childhood.

Herbert Sondheim: "A little saying for children on someone's birthday, little children particulary, that reminds me on my youth. We used to bring a flower or something and then we would stand and say: Ich bin klein, mein Wunsch ist klein, Mama, du sollst glücklich sein. Translate it? I am small, my wish is small, mother, you should be...(hesitates)... happy. Anyhow, it rhymes. Many of the German little sayings always (were) in form of rhymes. That's where the mainstay of their culture left them."

Obviously, he no longer identifies with the Germans, but this doesn't keep him from making fun of those who were born in the United States.

Herbert Sondheim: „Mum comes in and says she can't close the garage door. So I go out and... one, two, three, the very simple procedure. So I tell David: Die Eingeborenen saaachen (sagen), sie sind Affen, sodass sie nichts zu tun brauchen. Translated it means: The natives say they are monkeys, so they don't have to do any work. That applies here, too. Till next time!

It is audible that Herbert Sondheim enjoyed speaking his mother's and father's tongue, German with a Hessian accent, and also some words of Yiddish.

Herbert Sondheim: „Okay, I have the next time. On the departure of guests it is commonly said that bei dè größte Simkhe sinn (sind) die Gäst' nicht da. In other words: After they left, that's the biggest simkhe. David says the equivalent for that is: Everybody brings joy, some when they come, some when they go. I say (laughs): Mostly when they go. So much for that!"

In 2015, Herbert Sondheim died. Robin Smolen shares a loving memory: "Daddy was a special person. He was a loving son who respected and cared for his parents. He was a loving brother who on occasion created some mischief. He collected postage stamps, liked doing jigsaw puzzles and loved potatoes, although sometimes he was not allowed to eat them because he ate too many. He was a devoted husband and father and always provided for his family. He had three daughters, six grandchildren, and four great grandchildren, yet later in life he was referred to as 'grandpa' by hundreds of people. Every time he met a friend of one of his grandchildren or children they instantly felt a warm familiar connection with him. He had a wonderful sense of humor and a twinkle in his eye and a natural way of making everyone feel at ease. He was a great storyteller, and had many stories to tell about his exciting life and world travels. The importance to him of family, religion, hard work, integrity, humor and enthusiasm for life left a great legacy."

A Sabbath song, played by Veronika Bloemers during the presentation of Lastoria's audio book "Yiddish Live" in the Hohhaus Museum Lauterbach, Hesse, in 2019.

Many Americans of German descent ate what tasted like home. The potatoes Herbert Sondheim from Upper Hesse loved too much, were also served frequently in the family of Klezmer artist Yale Strom who was born in Detroit and has ancestors in Germany as well as in Eastern Europe. He lives and teaches in San Diego. Together with his wife, the Klezmer singer Elizabeth Schwartz from New York, he often tours through Europe. In the old Synagogue of Ober-Gleen, he has given a concert in 2017, with guitar player Nikolai Muck from Frankfurt/Main. Yale Strom is not only a great violinist, but also a charismatic entertainer who introduces his audience to authentic Jewish culture, language and traditions. As in the potato, pardon, bulbes song. He learned it "over the table", as he says, from his grandma who was from Ukraine. The German word for potato is Kartoffel.

Bulbes Song, Yale Strom (San Diego, violin and singing) and Nikolai Muck (Frankfurt/Main, guitar), in the former Synagogue of Ober-Gleen in 2017.

One of Herbert Sondheim's six grandchildren, Henry Smolen, has a high reputation in music: Henry Smolen, the son of Robin and Stuart Smolen, had started to play piano at the age of three in 2001 and gave his first public performance in San Jose, CA, when he was five years old. A veteran of the concert stage, he has performed all over the United States, making his orchestral debut at 8 years old with the El Camino Youth Symphony in Palo Alto, California. His performances include recitals at Carnegie Hall in New York, the Kimmel Center in Philadelphia, the Monterey Next Generation Jazz Festival, and at many well-known festivals. Henry Smolen was admitted to the San Francisco Conservatory of Music when he was 8 years old and has received a Master of Music degree in piano performance at the Juilliard School in New York City. The piece he is playing at the end of this podcast is the fourth movement of Beethoven's Piano Sonata No. 3, Op. 2. The sonata, often referred to as Beethoven's first virtuosic piano sonata, was composed in 1795 and was dedicated to Joseph Haydn.[7]

In 1939, when family Sondheim has arrived in the U.S., 83 percent of all Americans were opposed to taking in more Jewish refugees. Senator Robert Wagner and Representative Edith Rogers form a rescue committee and try to bring 20,000 orphans to the United States with a bill, but the children are included in the quotas. Unlike other countries, there is no Kindertransport to the United States. Jewish Germans are suspected of being spies. And some influential anti-Semites in business circles, the State Department and other institutions are preventing the US from becoming a haven.

In 1940, President Roosevelt arranges for 3268 well-known people from science and art to receive special visas. Journalist Varian Fry goes to Marseille on behalf of Eleanor Roosevelt's Emergency Rescue Committee to rescue Jews.

---

[7] An audio, provided by Robin Smolen, part of the Ober-Gleen-project.

In 1941, the United States entered World War II, after the bombing of Pearl Harbor, December 7, 1941.

In 1942, migrant workers from Mexico are needed. The legal basis for this is being created.

In 1943, restrictions on immigration for Chinese are lifted. Anyone who comes from an enemy country has little chance of being accepted. The application form for a visa is almost five feet long and must be completed on both sides. Two guarantors are needed, each of whom must also provide two guarantors. Anyone who comes from Italy or the "Third Reich" and has not yet been naturalized is considered an enemy alien and must carry a pink identity card. The assets are frozen. Radios, cameras and weapons, have to be handed over to the authorities, and it is not uncommon for children to be separated from their parents.

From 1933 to 1945, 107,832 people immigrated to the United States from Germany and Austria.

In 1948, the Displaced Persons Act is passed, the first law in the United States specifically for refugees. 400,000 people uprooted during the Second World War are allowed to enter the country. Among them were the sisters Hilda and Karola Stern from Nieder-Ohmen, who had survived Auschwitz and had been in a DP Camp in Austria, as well as Bea Karp nee Stern from Lauterbach in Upper Hesse, all of them orphans since their parents had perished in the Holocaust. Beate Stern and her little sister Susie had been hidden by the Jewish children's rescue organisation OSE in France. The book "My Broken Doll" that she published together with her daughter Deborah Pappenheimer, is her legacy. In the U.S., Hilda Stern Cohen saw her much younger cousin Ruth Stern, her aunt and uncle from Nieder-Ohmen again. She moved to Baltimore where so many other Upper Hessians had settled since the 19th Century, when the Port of Baltimore was the second largest gateway to the U.S., one of the destinations for steamships from Bremen. 21-year-old Hilda Stern went on board in Bremerhaven in 1946. In Baltimore, Hilda married Werner Cohen, a survivor from Essen. They raised three daughters and had twelve grandchildren. Hilda worked as an educator and bore testimony, but only after her death in 1997, her husband found her Holocaust poems that she had written after the war. They were published later in Germany under the title "Genagelt ist meine Zunge" (Nailed is my tongue) and in the book "Words that burn in me. Faith. Values. Survival" that came out in 2008. Powerful poems, full of pain and loss and hope, like the one titled "Heimat"[*]. A word that means so much more to a German emigrant than fatherland, home or homecountry.

Heimat

Überall ist meine Heimat.
Überall mein rastlos Herz.
Überall sind meine Träume,
überall mit mir der Schmerz.
Überall kommen Nächte

---

[*] Quoted from the audio book, read by Lilli Schwethelm on http://www.leafproduction.de.

täglich gleich auf mich herab.
Überall ist eine Sehnsucht.
Überall find ich ein Grab.

Home

Everywhere is my home.
Everywhere my restless heart.
Everywhere are my dreams,
Everywhere the pain's with me.
Everywhere nights come
down on me day by day.
Everywhere is a longing.
Everywhere I find a grave.

Storyteller Gail Rosen from Baltimore who had made interviews with Hilda followed her traces in the documentary film "For tomorrow. Ich hoff auf morgen" in 2010, directed by Eve Rennebarth, produced in Europe und the U.S.

In 1950, in the midst of the Cold War, communists were denied immigration under the Internal Security Act. Over the next two decades, 790,000 people will emigrate from Germany to the United States.

In 1951, 36-year-old Ellen Knauff nee Raphael is finally allowed to take the ferry and to leave Ellis Island for good. For three long years she had been held on the island that had been, during WWII, turned into a camp for US-citizens of German, Austrian, Japanese or Italian descent. The Supreme Court had ruled against Ellen Knauff. Her

156

deportation had been stopped at the last minute. Several times, the international press had reported about the struggle of this former civil servant of the U.S. Army, and Ellen Knauff has published her memoires. In 2020, Time Magazine had written about her famous case under the headline "A Dark Side of Ellis Island's History". In her young life, Ellen Knauff had already moved to another country four times and changed her citizenship twice when she came to the U.S. In 1934, at the age of 19, she had married a Czech and had moved to Czechoslowakia. When the war started in 1939, she fled to England. For years, she worked for the Royal Air Force and after the war for the U.S. Army in Frankfurt/Main. In 1948 she married a U.S. citizen in Frankfurt: Her husband Kurt Knauff, a German by birth, is a veteran, working for adminstration of the U.S. army in Germany. Soon after the wedding, Ellen Knauff tries to emigrate to the U.S., following the invitation from the War Brides Act. But when she arrives on Ellis Island, she is declared a risk for national security and without any further explanations, access to the U.S. is denied. It is a shock, but Ellen Knauff is willing to fight. Finally she learns that she has been taken for a communist spy! It takes her a long time to prove that she is innocent. One of the crucial questions in her case: Is anyone who is not an American citizen, and hasn't formally entered the country, entitled to be protected by the constitution of the United States of America?[9]

---

[9] See „*United States ex rel. Knauff v. Shaughnessy*" on *Wikipedia,* but also Ellen Knauff's book "The Ellen Knauff Story", the article "It happened here" on the website https://www.nytimes.com/1952/03/30/archives and the article "Woman with a country" on https://time.com/archive/6607735/the-press

In 1952, the McCarran-Walter Act was passed. The category "race" must no longer be an exclusion criterion. At the same time, an ideological criterion is introduced, because we are in the era of the political witch hunt: anyone who wants to enter or immigrate to the United States may be turned away because of political views.

In 1954, Ellis Island is closed. The last of the approximately 12 million people who have passed through this station is the Norwegian Arne Peterssen, a 48-year-old sailor who has once again stayed longer than allowed in the United States and has therefore been interned. As genealogist Megan Smolenyak found out, Arne Peterssen was deported a year later. He died in 1981 in his hometown of Larvik in southern Norway.

In 1965, the Immigration and Nationality Act is amended. National quotas will be abolished.

In 1980, the Refugee Act comes into force. Those who want to flee from a country behind the Iron Curtain or from the Middle East are no longer given preferential treatment.

In 1986, during the Reagan era, the Immigration and Control Act comes into force. Illegals living in the U.S. since 1982 are covered by an amnesty. At the same time, employers who employ illegal workers are threatened with sanctions. Border controls on the border with Mexico will be tightened.

In 1990, immigration quotas will be extended.

In 1995, immigration will be limited to 675,000 per year, the majority, 480,000 in the context of family reunification, 140,000 jobseekers and 55,000 from countries from which few immigrants have been recorded so far.

Ellis Island has been a museum for decades, the Statue of Liberty is a World Heritage Site.

According to the 2020 census, "together, the English (46.6 million), German (45 million), and Irish (38.6 million) alone or in any combination populations made up over half of the White alone or in combination population" of the United States. About twelve percent of the U.S. citizens have roots in Germany. "How the United States Immigration System Works", is described in 2024 on the website of the American Immigration Council.

Among the Hessian refugees of the Nazi era who have written childhood memoirs is Paul Kester[10] aka Kleinstrass from Wiesbaden as well as Ruth Stern Glass Earnest from Diez upon Lahn who had fled together with her mother Johanna Stern née Lamm from Ober-Gleen, her father Louis Stern from Balduinstein and her brothers Hermann and Ernst Lothar.

They had to start anew from almost zero and like in many other immigrant families, the parents saw to it that their children got a good education. Hermann and Ruth went first to a nearby public school, the almost 15-year-old

---

[10] Paul Kester, My Early Life in Germany and Sweden. And www.thekesters.net.

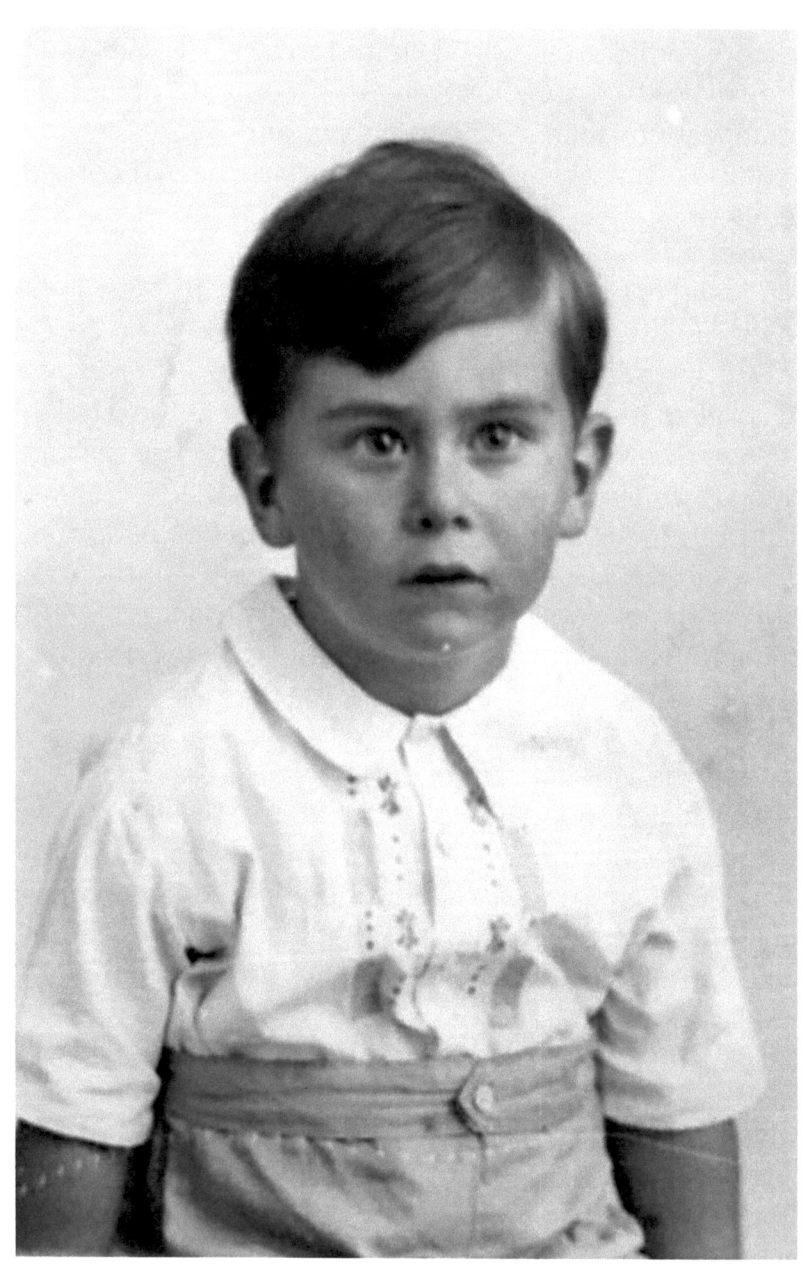

Ernst Lothar Stern from Diez upon Lahn.

Hermann into grade seven, and Ruth into grade one, instead of grade five. "A placement strategy to teach immigrant children English", she wrote in her memoir "The Gate". Ruth learned the meaning of the sight-words on flashcards, which taught her classmates to read. Their first names were Anglicized, but the parents still spoke some German and Yiddish.

Herman joined the U.S. Army and later the American military government in Germany, to help restart industry in what his family called the alte heimat (the old homeland), under the Marshall Plan. After his return he had a responsible position at General Electric. Ruth worked for decades as a teacher in New York and died in 2012. Her memoir "The Gate" that she has dedicated to her second husband, to her sons Abraham and David Glass, to her daughter-in-law Amy and her granddaughters Molly and Madeline has been translated into German. In 2016, two years before his death, her little brother, Ernst Lothar Stern, called Ernie, recounted his amazing career: "I was educated here in the United States, I was only almost four when we came here. Went to public schools. Graduated from high school. Went to a very good university called Cornell where I received a Bachelor of Science degree in economics. And worked in the electronics field all my working carreer. The job that I held longest and until I retired was with the French electronics and defense contractor then called Thomson CSF and currently called Thales, large corporation. I was the first American they hired, and I lived in New York City, in Manhattan. Our offices were in Manhattan. At first and then eventually, we began buying some companies in the

United States. I became chief executive officer (CEO) of the company. Worked with them for 41 years, retired in 2002."[11]

While reasons for global migration are not diminishing in the face of wars, climate change, famine, extreme poverty, oppression and persecution on political, cultural, racist, sexist and religious grounds, immigration becomes one of the main topics in political debates, in the U.S. as well as in Europe and other countries. More and more restrictions are demanded by extreme right-wings, but also by conservative parties. And if there is not a wall erected, populists call for the closing and control of once open borders, rejection, internment and deportation.

Donald Trump who is sworn in as U. S. President in January 2025 for the second time, plans "the largest deportation operation in American history" and intends to use the Alien Enemies Act from 1798, a law that allows the deportation of undocumented people from enemy nations during a time of war and played a role for the internment of Japanese during WWII.

Germany has gone from being a country of emigration to a country of refuge and still does not have an immigration policy worthy of the name.

Almost eight decades after her escape, Ruth Stern Gasten has returned to her home village Nieder-Ohmen one more time to present her childhood memories to a big audience. And on a pole, in front of the house of the

---

[11] Audio that Ernst (Ernie) Lothar Stern sent to the author. It is part of the audio book "Yiddish Life".

The childhood memoir of Ruth Stern Glass Earnest and the former family home in Diez.

protestant congregation, the reverend has hoisted the spangled banner. Introducing herself, Ruth speaks German, mixed with English and Hessian dialect: „Can everybody hear me? Okay, good! So: Ich sprech nicht mehr viel Deutsch, aber es freut mich sehr viel zu sein in Nieder-Ohmen, to be here in Nieder-Ohmen heut. Ich hab gesehen viele Leute, das hawwe mei' Familie gekennt, und... es ist gut für mei' Herz, my heart, hier zu sein." [12]

Warm applause fills the hall.

These are Ruth's words: "I don't speak much German anymore, but I'm very happy to be in Nieder-Ohmen, to be here in Nieder-Ohmen today. I saw a lot of people who knew my family, and it's good for my heart, mein Herz, to be here."

Ruth Stern Gasten is building bridges between people of different age, decent, opinion, religion or culture, and still hopes as her father Joseph Stern did that mankind is able to learn from the past. In 2019, there has been a rally of love in Livermore in the Tri Valley in California where she is living with her husband Sam Stone, family and friends. Ruth, a child survivor of the Holocaust, former refugee and Accidental American, who has founded an interfaith group and encouraged people to vote and to stand up for democracy, was asked to hold one of the speeches.

"My name is Ruth Gasten", she said. "I have the dubious distinction of entering the world's scene the same year as

---

[12] Audio from the event, by Justus Randt.

Ruth Stern Gasten (middle) and Sam Stone (left, in the back) in Nieder-Ohmen in 2017.

Adolf Hitler. He became chancellor of Germany and I was born in a tiny German village. My parents and I lived in a little cluster of farmhouses. As a small child I wandered from house to house, totally free. The front doors were open. I might help shell peas, sit next to a grandmother who was knitting and have her tell me a story or rub with the family dog. One day, the doors were closed. My mother told me it was because I was Jewish and Hitler had issued an edict: Christians were not to socialise with the Jews. I was confused and sad. But not everyone was intimidated. Soon, the heavy winter snow started falling. One snowy evening we heard a knock at the door. Our neighbor, Anna, stood there with her sled. 'As the Nazis keep me from sledding with Ruthie in the afternoon, lets go out now when no one is watching!' For the next two years, we went sledding in the moonlight. One of the few happy memories of my childhood. Fast forward to today. Like Anna, we are not intimidated. In the Tri Valley, we aren't shutting our doors on vulnerable people. We have a rally to say we honor diversity and value us all. I am happy to be part of it."[13]

At the end of the podcast, we hear Herbert Sondheim's grandson Henry Smolen, who was born in the United States in 1998, play Beethoven's Piano Sonata No. 3, Opus 2. This piece was recorded when he was a teenager.

---

[13] Audio sent to the author by Ruth Stern Gasten.

Bibliography

First Part: Out of necessity to America Hessian emigrants in the 19th and early 20th Century

Alsfelder Wochenblatt, 19th Century, from the archive of Ober-Gleen, Upper Hesse. English version: as translated by Monika Felsing with some help from Al and Susan Eldridge.

Alsfelder Zeitung, 19th Century, from the archive of Ober-Gleen. English version: as translated by Monika Felsing with some help from Al and Susan Eldridge.

Blaschka-Eick, Simone, „In die Neue Welt! Deutsche Auswanderer in drei Jahrhunderten", Rowohlt, Hamburg 2010. The author is the Director of the Deutsche Auswandererhaus, the German Emigration Center, Bremerhaven. Blaschka-Eick and Hermann Simon: Irene Stratenwert, „Der gelbe Schein. Mädchenhandel 1860 bis 1930", Bremerhaven 2012. Catalogue of an exhibition about female emigrants of the 19th and early 20th century. Especially about Hesse is the chapter „Im Goldrausch: Hessische Mädchen als ‚Hurdy-Gurdy-Girls'", pp. 27 ff.

Deutsche Gesellschaft der Stadt New York, German Society of the City of New York, Practical Advice and Information for Emigrants, Rathgeber für Auswanderungswillige, New York 1883. English version: as translated by Monika Felsing with some help from Al and Susan Eldridge.

Brüder Grimm, Kinder- und Haus-Märchen, Berlin 1819, p. 141. English version: as translated by Monika Felsing with some help from Al and Susan Eldridge.

Faber, Hartwig, Kleber, Carl and Bicker, Gudrun, „Auswanderungen aus Neustadt (Hessen) und tangierten Orten in der Umgebung nach Amerika in den Jahren 1830-1945", online on the website of Familienforschung Neustadt.
Felsing, Monika, Himmel un Höll, BOD, Norderstedt 2016.
Gillhoff, Johannes, Jürnjakob Swehn, der Amerikafahrer, 7. Auflage, München 2009. English version: as translated by Monika Felsing with some help from AI and Susan Eldridge.
Hailer-Schmidt, Annette: "Hier können wir ja nicht mehr leben. Hintergründe, Motive, Funktionen", published by the Kommission für deutsche und osteuropäische Volkskunde in der deutschen Gesellschaft für Volkskunde, Marburg 2004.
Helbich, Wolfgang, „Amerika ist ein freies Land... Auswanderer schreiben nach Deutschland", Darmstadt 1985.
Helbich, „Alle Menschen sind dort gleich". Die deutsche Amerika-Auswanderung im 19. und 20. Jahrhundert, Düsseldorf 1988.
Helbich und Walter D. Kamphoefner, Ulrike Sommer, Briefe aus Amerika. Deutsche Auswanderer schreiben aus der Neuen Welt 1830-1930, München 1988.
The same authors, News from the Land of Freedom. German Immigrants Write Home, Ithaca, Cornell UP 1991.
Hinze, Werner, "Hier hat man täglich seine Noth". Lieder von Auswanderern, Hamburg 2009.
Intelligenzblatt für den Kreis Alsfeld, 19th century, from the archive of Ober-Gleen. English version: as translated by Monika Felsing with some help from AI and Susan Eldridge.
Jochem, Marlene, „Aufbruch nach Amerika", publication of the Theodor-Zink-Museum, Heft 17, Kaiserslautern 2009. See information about Heinrich Georg from

Langenaubach, born in 1821, who emigrated in 1852, on https://www.kaiserslautern.de.

Knauf, Diethelm, and Barry Moreno, „Aufbruch in die Fremde. Migration gestern und heute", Bremen 2009. With DVD.

Knauf and Moreno, "Leaving Home, Migration Yesterday and Today", Bremen 2010.

Lemcke, Heinrich, „Canada, das Land und seine Leute. Ein Führer und geographisches Handbuch", Leipzig 1897. English version: as translated by Monika Felsing with some help from AI and Susan Eldridge.

Schott, Carolyn, "Yes you! Yes now! Visiting your Ancestral Town", Columbia Capstone, Seattle 2010.

Seim, Wolfgang, „Auswanderung aus dem Kirchspiel Maulbach", Mitteilungen des Geschichts- und Museumsvereins Alsfeld, January 2014. English version: as translated by Monika Felsing with some help from AI and Susan Eldridge.

Stölting, Siegfried, „Auswanderer auf alter Zeitungsgrafik", Worpswede 1987.

Urlen, Falk, „Juchheisa nach Amerika, ein Beitrag über hessische Söldner", online on https://www.erinnerungen-im-netz.de.

Volksliederarchiv, Müller-Lüdenscheidt-Verlag, by Michael Zachcial et al., https://www.volksliederarchiv.de. Michael Zachcial and the group „Grenzgänger" have a high reputation.

Weitershaus, Friedrich Wilhelm, „Wir ziehen nach Amerika", MOHG 63, 1978, pp. 185 ff., online on http://geb.uni-giessen.de.

Second Part: Departure to freedom

Of 500 who set out to find and fight for human rights. Some of them have changed the country they settled in to the better

Addresses In Memory Of Carl Schurz, Address of Professor Eugene Kühnemann, New York Committee of the Carl Schurz Memorial, New York 1906, S. 24.

Bergerson, Andrew Stuart und Logge, Thorsten, German Migration to Missouri. A Transnational Student Research Project, published by the Landeszentrale für Politische Bildung, Hamburg, 2019. Online on https://www.ge-schichte.uni-hamburg.de.

Der deutsche Pionierverein von Cincinnati, Der deutsche Pionier, Ohio 1872.

Follenius, Paul, und Münch, Friedrich, „Aufforderung und Erklärung in Betreff einer Auswanderung im Großen aus Teutschland in die nordamerikanischen Freistaaten", zweite Auflage, Gießen 1833. Online for example on https://rosdok.uni-rostock.de. English version: as translated by Monika Felsing with some help from AI and Susan Eldridge.

DeWitt, Petra, Der Staat Missouri, Friedrich Münch's German-American Perception of and Guides to Missouri, 1859-1875, Yearbook of German-American Studies 45 (2010), pp. 17 ff. Thanks to Jim Münch for the hint.

Duden, Gottfried, Bericht über eine Reise nach den westlichen Staaten Nordamerika's und einen mehrjährigen Aufenthalt am Missouri (in den Jahren 1824, 25, 26 und 1827), in Bezug auf Auswanderung und Uebervölkerung,

Elberfeld 1829. English version: as translated by Monika Felsing with some help from AI and Susan Eldridge.

Gillhoff, Johannes, Jürnjakob Swehn der Amerikafahrer, 7th edition, München 2009.

Dirk Hoerder, Geschichte der deutschen Migration vom Mittelalter bis heute, München 2010.

Horst, Corinna, „More than ordinary...": The female migration experience and German immigrant women in nineteenth century Cincinnati, Diss. Miami University, 1998.

Muehl, Siegmar, Shock of the New: Advising Mid-Nineteenth-Century German Immigrants to Missouri, Yearbook of German American Studies 33, 1988, pp. 85-101. Thanks to Jim Muench for the hint.

Muench Family Association, https://www.muenchfamily-association.com.

Münch, Friedrich, Gesammelte Schriften, St. Louis 1902. The book is online, on archive.org. English versions of German publications of Münch: as translated by Monika Felsing with some help from AI and Susan Eldridge.

Münch, Speech, July 4, 1840, Coll. AO747, Immigration to Missouri Collection (IMC). St. Louis: Missouri History Museum Archives. Quoted as by Alexander Banks und Michael Spachek, German Americans and Slavery in: Bergerson und Logge, German Migration to Missouri, pp. 14 ff.

Münch, Opfer für die gute Sache, published on September 1, 1861, quoted as in Utopia, pp. 222 f.

Münch, Erinnerungen aus Deutschlands trübster Zeit, dargestellt in den Lebensbildern von Karl Follen, Paul Follen und Friedrich Münch, St. Louis (Missouri) und Neustadt a.d. Haardt 1873.

Münch, Der Staat Missouri, geschildert mit besonderer Rücksicht auf teutsche Einwanderung, C. Hauser, New York, 1859. Later editions: Der Staat Missouri. Ein Handbuch für deutsche Auswanderer. Mit einem Anhange, mehreren Abbildungen und der neuesten Karte des Staates Missouri. 3., den neuesten Verhältnissen entsprechend und ganz umgearbeitete und ansehnlich vermehrte Auflage, Tannen, Bremen 1875. See https://digital.staatsbibliothek-berlin.de.

Münch, A treatise on religion and christianity, orthodoxy and rationalism. An appeal to the common-sense of all who like truth better than. B. H. Greene, Boston 1847.

Münch, American Grape Culture. Brief But Thorough and Practical Guide to the Laying Out of Vineyards, the Treatment of Vines, and the Production of Wine in North America. Conrad Witter, St. Louis, Missouri 1859.

Münch, Amerikanische Weinbauschule, St. Louis 1877.

Münch, "On the Position and Rights of Women." Channing, William Henry, ed. The Spirit of the Age, vol. I, no. 18, Sat., 11/3/1848, p. 283. Duplicated in: Woman's Place is in the History Books, Her Story: 1620-1980: A Civic Guide for American History Teachers.

Münch, James F., https://www.jamesfmuench.com. Material about his ancestor who had published under the alias „Far West".

Münch, James F., Anita M. Mallinckrodt, Marc Houseman und Cathie Schoppenhorst, The Historic 1830s German Immigration to Missouri, Missouri 2016.

Münch, Pauline, Aus dem Familienbericht von Pauline Münch. Collection of Marilyn H. Merrit. Transcribed by Rolf Schmidt. Quoted as by Rohrbach, Rita.

Olshausen, Theodore, Der Staat Missouri, geographisch und statistisch beschrieben; also Karte des Staats Missouri nach den besten Hülfsmitteln bearbeitet, Akademische Buchhandlung, Kiel 1854.

Reisende Sommerrepublik und Stadtarchiv Gießen, Utopia. Aufbruch in die Utopie, Bremen 2013.

Rohrbach, Rita, Bleiben oder gehen. Die Gießener Auswanderungsgesellschaft. Ein Schülerheft für die Sekundarstufe in der Reihe Schülerhefte zur Geschichte Gießens, Gießen 2013.

Schelbitzki Pickle, Linda, "German-Speaking Women in Nineteenth Century Missouri: The Immigrant Experience", in Whites, LeeAnn et al., Women in Missouri History, University of Missouri Press, 2004, pp. 42-63.

Schelbitzki Pickle, Contented Among Strangers, Rural German Speaking Women and Their Families in the Nineteenth Century Midwest, University of Illinois Press, 1996.

Schelbitzki Pickle, Stereotypes and Reality: Nineteenth-Century German Women in Missouri, in: Missouri Historical Review 79, 1985, pp. 291-312.

Schmidt, Rolf, Die Gießener Auswanderungsgesellschaft. Vom Scheitern einer deutschen Republik, in MOHG 5, 2010, S. 77 ff. See http://geb.uni-giessen.de. Rolf Schmidt from Bremen-Borgfeld is also the author of a trilogy about the Giessener Emigration Society and was part of the Reisende Sommerrepublik.

Schröder, Gustav, Heimatlos auf Hoher See: Bericht vom Kapitän der St. Louis, Berlin 1949, that was put online by Hape Etzold.

Schubert, Cornelius, Tagebuch von 1834, transcribed by Jürgen Schmitz and Rolf Schmidt, published in Rohrbach,

Rita, Bleiben oder gehen. The diary is part of the Schubert Family Papers, Western Historical Manuscript Collection, Columbia, Missouri.

Schurz, Carl, "True Americanism", Address, Faneuil Hall, Boston (18 April 1859) in: Speeches of Carl Schurz, J.B. Lippincott and Co., Philadelphia: 1865, archive.org, published as on https://falschzitate.blogspot.com.

Smith, Ursula and Peavy, Linda, Pioneer Women. The Lives of Women on the Frontier, Glasgow, Scotland, 1986.

Smith and Peavy, Westwärts mit gerafften Röcken. Pionierinnen in Nordamerika. Verlag Gerstenberg, Hildesheim 2012.

Treu, Georg, Ratgeber für Auswanderungswillige, 1848. English version: as translated by Monika Felsing with some help from AI and Susan Eldridge.

Vieth, Richard, Adventure into Hope: the Founding and Fate of the Giessen Emigration Society and its Organizers Friedrich Muench and Paul Follenius,

Volksliederarchiv, Müller-Lüdenscheidt-Verlag, Michael Zachcial, https://www.volksliederarchiv.de.

Warren County Historical Society, Friedrich Muench and the Giessen Emigration Society's role in Missouri still visible today.

Weitershaus, Friedrich Wilhelm, „Wir ziehen nach Amerika. Ein Beitrag zur oberhessischen Auswanderung im 19. Jahrhundert, MOHG 63, 1978, pp. 185-201. This is online.

Third Part: Zweiback and Captain's Dinner

How a five-year-old and a seventeen-year-old from Hesse experienced their first sea voyage and what became of them and others

Asterita, Ida Hase, Letters From Edmund, as translated by Ida (Hase) Asterita, badmorgen.wordpress.com. The original is lost.

Berg, Gustav Freiherr von, An meine Lieben in der Heimat. Reisebriefe aus Nord-Amerika vom 25. Juli bis 28. November 1893, Wien 1894. Online on archive.org. Translated by Monika Felsing with some help from Al and Susan Eldridge.

Cohen, Hilda Stern, Genagelt ist meine Zunge. Published in cooperation with Werner V. Cohen by Erwin Leibfried, Sascha Feuchert and William Gilcher, Bergauf-Verlag, Frankfurt/Main 2003, as volume 2 of Memento, a series of publications of the Ernst-Ludwig-Chambré-Stiftung, Lich, and the Arbeitsstelle Holocaustliteratur of the Justus-Liebig-Universität Gießen. See part 6 of the podcast.

Felsing, Monika, "Ja, wir schweben", lyrics, published in one of her songbooks.

Fittkau, Tanja, „Vom zusätzlichen Frachtgut zum umworbenen Kunden. Die Überfahrtsbedingungen für Seereisende und ihre Grenzerfahrungen 1830-1932", published by the German Emigration Center, Deutsches Auswandererhaus, Bremerhaven 2020.

Gasten, Ruth Stern, An Accidental American, Xlibris, Corp., 2010.

Gasten, Zufällig Amerikanerin, BOD, translated by Monika Felsing, Norderstedt 2017.

Kofahl, Jens, Deutsche Gesellschaft zur Rettung Schiffbrüchiger (DGzRS, German Society for the Rescue of Shipwrecked Persons), on https://www.seenotretter.de/magazin. English version: as translated by Monika Felsing with some help from AI and Susan Eldridge.

Lemcke, Heinrich, „Canada, das Land und seine Leute. Ein Führer und geographisches Handbuch, Leipzig 1897". English version: as translated by Monika Felsing with some help from AI and Susan Eldridge.

Schmittborn, Lydia, "Zwei Brüder wollten wandern (Untergang der Cimbria)", Espa 1883. English version: as translated by Monika Felsing with some help from AI and Susan Eldridge. The melody is a traditional, "Wer lieben will, muss leiden", till 1900 also the melody of "Mein Hut, der hat drei Ecken".

Silcher, Friedrich, "Muss i denn zum Städtele hinaus", Schwaben (Deutschland), Svabia (Germany), 1827.

Simon, Herbert, „Die Auswanderung von Bürgern aus Hessen insbesondere aus der Stadt und dem ehemaligen Kreis Melsungen nach Nordamerika im 19. Jahrhundert", S. 218 ff., online on http://www.vhghessen.de and https://www.archiv-melsungen.de.

Unknown Author, "Der Untergang der Cimbria", poem about 1883, as translated by Monika Felsing with some help from AI and Susan Eldridge, to be found online in the Volksliederarchiv.

Vollrath, Paul, "Heute an Bord", Sailor's song, 19th Century, as translated by Monika Felsing with some help from AI and Susan Eldridge, composer unknown, 1903.

Fourth Part: A home far away from home

Emigration becomes immigration. Hessian contributions to American history of the 17th and 18th centuries

Ashbaugh, Carolyn, Lucy Parsons. An American Revolutionary, 2013.

Asmus, Georg, Amerikanisches Skizzebüchelche, Zwei Episteln in Versen in hessischer Mundart, 1. Epistel: Wissmer & Rogers News Co., New York 1874 2. Aufl. und 2. Epistel : Vlg. V. Eduard Heinrich Mayer Cöln und Leipzig 1876.

Brandt, Armin M., Bau deinen Altar in fremder Erde, Jahre Germantown. Stuttgart. 1983. On https://angekommen. com you find quotations from this book under „Route Migration Erinnerungsort Pastorius-Denkmal Krefeld.

Gräf, Holger Th., Ein oberhessischer Hirtensohn beim „Letzten Mohikaner". George Schneider aus Fellingshausen im „French and Indian War" (1754-63) und die transatlantischen seiner Familie bis zur Mitte des 19. Jahrhunderts, in: Mitteilungen des Oberhessischen Geschichtsvereins Gießen 101 (2016), pp. 121-142.

Herder, Hans, Hessisches Auswandererbuch. Berichte, Chroniken und Dokumente zur Geschichte hessischer Einwanderer in den Vereinigten Staaten 1683-1983. Ein hessischer Beitrag zum 300. Jahrestag der ersten deutschen Einwanderung in Amerika, Frankfurt/M. 1983.

Leggewie, Claus, Germany as an Immigrant Country, in Knauf/Moreno, Leaving Home (siehe Bibliographie Part I), S. 241 ff.

Lemcke, Heinrich, Abfertigung in Castle Gardens, Husumer Wochenblatt, Mai 1886, zitiert nach Pauseback, Paul-Heinz,

Übersee-Auswanderer aus Schleswig-Holstein. Husum 2000, p. 91.

Nuhn, Heinrich: August Spiess - Ein hessischer Sozialrevolutionär in Amerika, Winfried Jenior, 2000, https://www.museum-friedewald.de.

Parsons, Lucy, Life of Albert R. Parsons, Chicago 1889.

Wepmann, Dennis, The Swinging Door – Changing Patterns in Contemporary American Immigration, in: Knauf/Moreno, Leaving Home (siehe Bibliographie Part 1), pp. 231 ff.

Fifth Part: In the light of Lady Liberty's Torch.

How immigrants experienced their arrival on Ellis Island

Holleufer, Henriette von, Between Nowhere and Somewhere: One Displaced Person's Odyssey to Freedom, in: Knauf/Moreno, Leaving Home (siehe Bibliographie Part 1), pp. 219 ff.

Lemcke Heinrich, Einwanderer auf Ellis Island, Die Gartenlaube, Leipzig 1897, Heft 40, pp. 666-669.

Tebbens, Christoph, diary on https://www.heimatmuseum-leer.de. Projektpartner: Heimatverein Leer e. V. – Heimatmuseum Leer, Western Michigan University Archives & Regional History Collections, family Burmeister, Recklinghausen, Ostfriesische Landschaft Aurich.

Wüstenbecker, Katja, Deutsch-Amerikaner im Ersten Weltkrieg. US-Politik und nationale Identitäten im Mittleren Westen, Steiner Verlag, 2007.

Sixth Part: Welcome Or Not Welcome?

A fearful question. How the conditions of immigration to the United States have changed since the early 20th Century

Felsing, Monika, Himmel un Höll, BOD, Norderstedt 2016.
Felsing, audiobook „Yiddish Life", 2018.
Karp, Bea, and Pappenheimer, Deborah, „My Broken Doll". There is also a play under this title. See also https://ihene.org/nebraska-survivor-stories/bea-karp.
Schweitzer, Eva, Amerika und der Holocaust. Die verschwiegene Geschichte, München 2004.
Wichmann, Manfred, Nothing Saved but His Own Life – The Banishment and Flight of the Jewish Lawyer Karl Rosenthal from Nazi-Germany, in: Knauf/Moreno, Leaving Home (see Bibliographie Part I), pp. 211 ff.

Credits

Podcast "Now we go...Overseas"

Written by, and final technical editing: Monika Felsing, Bremen, Germany.
English version directed by: Susan Eldridge, nee Badenhausen, Connecticut, USA.
Recordings by Susan Eldridge, Justus Randt, Monika Felsing and some of the readers.
Copyright: in Connecticut (United States), and in Bremen (Germany), 2023, 2024 and 2025.

Lastoria wishes to thank all the readers, musicians and singers who participated in this podcast.

Part I:

Theme "Now we go... Overseas" (Intro and extro, melody): Burghard Bock, Bremen, und Monika Felsing, Bremen and Ober-Gleen, Germany.
Theme "Now we go Overseas...": first stanza, audience of a singing workshop on October 6, 2023, in Ober-Gleen, with Monika Felsing. Solo recording: Niki Rittenhouse.
First Narrator: Susan Eldridge, nee Badenhausen, Connecticut, USA.
Second Narrator: Thomas Fulton, Connecticut, USA, who also read the Hessian Soldiers' poem, and the beginning of the Bremen Town Musician story.
Friedrich Jacob Wichelhausen: Thoralv Dunkel in Bremen, Germany, who also read the Alsfeld Newspaper segments.
Catharina (Lanz) Büttner: Monika Felsing, who also read three poems: the first about the female emigrant, the second about Germans remaining in their homeland, and the third about the Germans preparing to leave.
Walter Ruppenthal: Douglas Eldridge in Connecticut, USA, who also read Jurnjakob Swehn, Georg Fett and Heinrich Lemcke's Golden Rules for Emigrants.
The German Society of the City of New York: Regina Dietzold in Bremen, Germany
Georg Treu: Joseph Garms in Connecticut, USA.
Di grine Kuzine (The Green Cousin) was performed by Burghard Bock in Bremen, Germany.

The final song, Go Away, Come Back (Gieh foadd, komm werre), was performed by Monika Felsing and the audience in Ober-Gleen in 2018. The lyrics in translation, written by Monika Felsing: Go away, come back, go away, come back, even if you don't stay. What binds you to a place are the people, also those who don't live anymore. The nature – vulnerable. The houses – destroyable. It would be a lie to say it didn't matter. Go away, come back, go away, come back, even if you don't stay. You know that clocks might stand still if you don't wind them up or if they are out of order. But the time never sleeps. Go away, come back, go away, come back – something of you stays here.

Part 2:

Theme "Now we go... Overseas" (Intro and extro, melody): Burghard Bock, Bremen, and Monika Felsing, Bremen and Ober-Gleen, Germany.
"Brüder, so kann's nicht gehen" and „Die Gedanken sind frei": „Duo EigenArt", Helmut Brück and Kirsten Ludanek, Nidderau, Germany.
Narrator: Susan Eldridge, Connecticut, USA, who also read the English translations of the lyrics „Brothers, it can't go like this" and "Thoughts are free".
Paul Follenius: Hans-Peter Klein, Melsungen, Germany.
Friedrich Münch: Leslie Krieke, Connecticut, USA.
Carl Schurz: Monika Felsing, Bremen and Ober-Gleen, Germany, who also read the part of Maria Follenius and

sang "Woas dir käis duh soll" (What no one should do to you).
Hoffmann von Fallersleben: Ingrid Ruscheinski, Bremen, Germany.
Cornelius Schubert: Lucien McRobbie, Chicago, USA.
Gottfried Duden: Reinhard Jung, Ritterhude, Germany.
Georg Treu: Burghard Bock, Bremen, Germany.
Pauline Münch: Dorris Keeven-Franke, Missouri, USA.
„Sisters, it can't go like this" sung by Niki Rittenhouse, Connecticut, USA.
Jürnjakob Swehn: Peter Valtink, Bremen, Germany.
Ruth Stern Gasten: Livermore, California, USA.

Part 3

Theme "Now we go... Overseas" (Intro and extro, melody): Burghard Bock, Bremen, and Monika Felsing, Bremen and Ober-Gleen, Germany.
„Heute an Bord": Shanty Chor Bremen-Mahndorf, a chanty choir in Bremen, Germany.
Introduction and some poems: Susan Badenhausen Eldridge, Connecticut, USA.
Narrator: Cimbria Badenhausen, Connecticut, USA.
Edmund Badenhausen: John Badenhausen, USA.
Ida Hase Astarita: Cintra Olson, nee Badenhausen, in Connecticut, USA.
"We hover": Monika Felsing, Bremen, Germany.
Physician: Lucien McRobbie, Chicago, USA.
Heinrich Lemcke: Reinhard Jung, Bremen, Germany.

Gustav Freiherr von Berg was read by Burghard Bock in Bremen, Germany.

„Muss ech dann", the Upper Hessian translation of the Swabian folk song "Muss i denn": Lyrics read by Helga Felsing, in Bremen, Germany.

Part 4

Theme "Now we go... Overseas" (Intro and extro, melody): Burghard Bock, Bremen, and Monika Felsing, Bremen and Ober-Gleen, Germany.

Poem by Emma Lazarus: Erika Thies, Worpswede, Germany.

Narrator: Susan Eldridge, Connecticut, USA.

Accordion: Laura Schneider from Kirtorf and her grandfather in the church of Ober-Gleen, Germany, in 2014.

Timeline: Ingo Behrens, Rolf (Rollo) Schmidt, Monika Felsing, Christel Schipmann, Kritika Thapa in Bremen, Germany.

Franz Pastorius: Thoralv Dunkel, Bremen, Germany.

"Mir sai all Geschwisder": Upper Hessian coversong to the melody of „O mio babbino caro" (Puccini), lyrics by Monika Felsing sung by a project choir in a benefit concert for „Reporters without Borders" at the Alsfelder Kulturtage in Alsfeld, Germany. At the piano, leading the concert: Veronika Bloemers. Project choir: Hans-Peter Klein, Bianca Haarich, Arnulf Triebel, Helmut Meß, Elisabeth Wagner, Regina Weller, Peter Jerabeck, Claudia Munsch, Monika Felsing, Anna Thum and Rebekka Bachmann.

"Panis Angelicus": sung by Gabriele Gonder Carey, USA.

George Schneider: Rolf (Rollo) Schmidt, Bremen, Germany.

Part 5

Theme "Now we go... Overseas" (Intro and extro, melody): Burghard Bock, Bremen, and Monika Felsing, Bremen and Ober-Gleen, Germany.
Narrator: Susan Eldridge, nee Badenhausen, Connecticut, USA.
Heinrich Lemcke: Reinhard Jung, Ritterhude.
Timeline: Ingo Behrens, Rolf (Rollo) Schmidt in Bremen, Germany.
Christoph Tebbens and stuttering mother: Monika Felsing, Bremen, Germany.
Immigration Officer and father: Thoralv Dunkel, Bremen, Germany.
Judge: Hans Ganten, Worpswede, Germany.
Russian Jew: Erika Thies, Worpswede, Germany.
Interpreter: Horst Rasch, Worpswede, Germany.
Innkeeper's Wife, crying mother and American woman: Regina Dietzold, Bremen, Germany.
Klezmer Improvisation: Yale Strom, San Diego, USA, and Clive Ford, Edna Eversmeier, Till Eversmeier and David Hodgkinson of the Klezmer group "Cladatje", Ortrud Staude, Burghard Bock of the Klezmer group "Para-dawgma" and Thomas Stapke at a Klezmer workshop taught by Yale Strom in March 2019 in Bremen, Germany.

Part 6

Theme "Now we go... Overseas" (Intro and extro, melody): Burghard Bock, Bremen, and Monika Felsing, Bremen and Ober-Gleen.

First Narrator: Susan Eldridge nee Badenhausen, Connecticut, USA.

Second Narrator: Monika Felsing, Bremen, Germany.

Timeline: Horst Rasch, Erika Thies and Hans Ganten (Worpswede), Reinhard Jung (Ritterhude), Peter Kühlborn (Ober-Ramstadt), Christine Renken, Beruta Adolf, Jürgen Moser, Justus Randt and Monika Felsing (Bremen), who also read the poem „Heimat" by Hilda Stern Cohen.

Robin Smolen, California, USA.

Herbert Sondheim, USA, recording from the Seventies.

Albert Stern: Joachim Hahn, webmaster of Alemannia Judaica, Germany. Alemannia Judaica is a rich source of information to be found online. There are pages about a lot of German villages and towns and German-Jewish history, mostly, but not only about Southern Germany.

Ernst Lothar Stern, USA, recording from 2016.

Ruth Stern Gasten, Livermore, California, USA.

„Bulbes Song": Yale Strom (San Diego, violine) and Nikolai Muck (Frankfurt upon Main, guitar), in 2017 in the former Synagogue of Ober-Gleen.

„Es Kälbche", Upper Hessian coversong of „Dona Dona" or „Dos Kelbl" by Shlomo Secunda (1940), sang by the project choir at the benefit concert for „Reporters without Borders" at the Alsfelder Kulturtage in 2022, with Hans-Peter Klein, Bianca Haarich, Arnulf Triebel, Helmut Meß, Elisabeth Wagner, Regina Weller, Peter Jerabeck, Claudia Munsch, Monika Felsing, Anna Thum and Rebekka Bachmann.

"Saa, kennsde mech": Upper Hessian coversong of Auld Lang Syne. written by Monika Felsing, sang with the audience in a singing workshop in the former Synagogue of Ober-Gleen in 2019.

Klezmer Improvisation: Yale Strom, San Diego, USA, and Clive Ford, Edna Eversmeier, Till Eversmeier and David Hodgkinson of the Klezmer group "Cladatje", Ortrud Staude, Burghard Bock of the Klezmer group "Paradawgma" and Thomas Stapke at a Klezmer workshop taught by Yale Strom in March 2019 in Bremen, Germany.

Sabbath Song: Veronika Bloemers in the Hohhaus Museum, Lauterbach, Hesse in 2018, during the presentation of the audio book "Yiddish Life".

Beethoven's Piano Sonate no. 3, Opus 2, played by Henry Smolen, a grandson of Herbert Sondheim from Ober-Gleen.

Image and text rights

The photos in this book have been shared with us by family Badenhausen, Linda Silverman-Shefler, Carolyn Schott, Robin Smolen nee Sondheim, family Ruppenthal, family Gonder, Ruth Stern Gasten, Monika Felsing and Justus Randt. We have made every effort to clarify image and text rights. If we have infringed upon any rights, we would ask the copyright holders to contact us. The materials have been processed for non-profit use and our historical society, Lastoria e.V., Bremen, is not pursuing any commercial purposes with this voluntary project.

Contact

If you wish to contact our historical society Lastoria, Bremen, just send a message to mail(at)lastoria-bremen. de. You find the podcast and information on our voluntary work in my blog on www.monikafelsing.de.

Epilogue

This was an experience, if not an adventure. When we started the podcast project in Bremen, we would never have thought it would become something bigger. But then, in all these years of voluntary work for our Historical Society Lastoria, named after the once famous variety theatre Astoria (1908-1968), Bremen, we had never known what our work would lead to. It is always a travel to the unknown, to shores we haven't heard of, yet. And that's part of the motivation.

In all of our projects, we are preserving memories and bringing people together. We cooperate with researchers and institutions, and we share the results of our voluntary work with the public, in books, in audio books, in my blog, in speeches, workshops and this podcast. Without doubt, the past has an influence on our own time and on the future, and there is more to learn than one has ever dreamed of. It is a journey, and there is no return – as we ourselves change while we dedicate ourselves to a work like this. A work that has to do with human rights and democracy, a work that is connected to the question how we treat each other and what we expect of life.

Ideals are like stars – they really are. And while we, too, are setting our course according to them, we can learn a lot about ourselves and about others. If it goes well, we learn to listen again, to reflect what we hear and to act humanly. This adventure never ends. You are welcome to join it.

Monika Felsing, Historical Society Lastoria, Bremen
Spring 2025